UNEARTHING

· THE ·

SECRET

GARDEN

THE SECRET GARDEN

BY FRANCES
HODGSON BURNETT
ILLUSTRATED BY
CHARLES ROBINSON

WILLIAM HEINEMANN
21 BEDFORD STREET
LONDON · W·C · 1911 ·

Title page from the first London edition of *The Secret Garden*.

To Andrea,

UNEARTHING

· THE ·

SECRET GARDEN

THE PLANTS AND PLACES THAT
INSPIRED FRANCES HODGSON BURNETT

Happy retirement!

MARTA MCDOWELL

Marta McDowell

TIMBER PRESS · PORTLAND, OREGON

2022

Published by Timber Press, Inc.
The Haseltine Building
133 S.W. Second Avenue, Suite 450
Portland, Oregon 97204-3527
timberpress.com

Printed in China

MIX
Paper from responsible sources
FSC® C104723
www.fsc.org

"An American Author's English Ha-ha," originally published in *Country Life in America*, vol. 10, no. 3, copyright 1906 by Doubleday, Page & Company, New York.
My Robin, copyright 1912 by Frederick A. Stokes Company, New York.
In the Garden, copyright 1924 by Curtis Publishing Company, Philadelphia, and 1925, The Medici Society of America, Boston and New York.
Cover design by Dylan Mierzwinski
Text design by Stacy Wakefield Forte

ISBN 978-1-60469-990-6

Catalogue records for this book are available from the Library of Congress and the British Library.

·

FOR EVERYONE
WHO HAS LOVED,
LOVES, OR WILL
LOVE *THE SECRET
GARDEN*.

·

It was a lovesome, mystic place, shut in partly by old red brick walls against which fruit trees were trained and partly by a laurel hedge with a wood behind it. It was my habit to sit and write there under an aged writhen tree, gray with lichen and festooned with roses.

—From *My Robin* (1912), describing the rose garden at Maytham Hall

Frances Hodgson Burnett posing with her sundial and roses in the garden that inspired *The Secret Garden.*

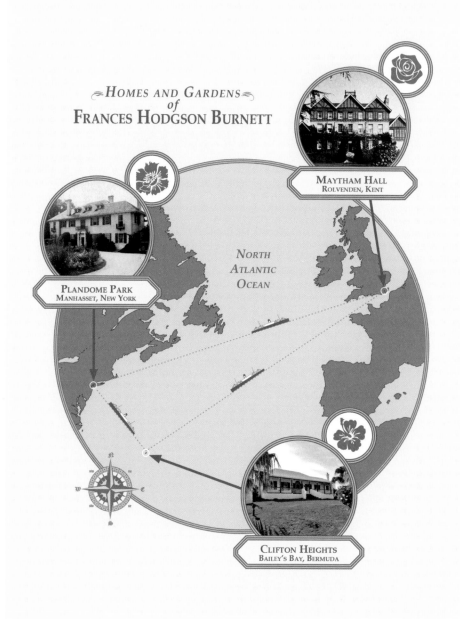

The three homes and gardens of Frances Hodgson Burnett.

CONTENTS

Mary Lennox at the door of the secret garden, illustrated by Tasha Tudor.

C AN A BOOK be a horticultural trigger? A sort of gateway drug for gardeners? If so, then surely *The Secret Garden*
by Frances Hodgson Burnett is a contender. A friend of mine—Jane
Taylor—credited the book with her lifelong pursuit of gardening.
When she was eight or nine years old, Jane contracted a severe case of
chicken pox, complicated by pneumonia. These were the days before
antibiotics, as she reminded me, and she spent most of that school
year in bed. Every day her mother read aloud one chapter of *The
Secret Garden*, an antidote to the boredom of the sickroom. Jane fell
in love with the story that unlocked a dream of bringing plants and
gardens to life, a dream of recovery.

Were Burnett still with us, she would be puzzled and perhaps amused by the state of her reputation today, nearly one hundred years after her death. She was an unlikely garden writer—particularly for inspiring children—as she did not cultivate any substantial bit of earth until she was on the doorstep of her fiftieth birthday. Her output of juvenile fiction was small in comparison to her otherwise prodigious body of work. Yet of her fifty-plus novels, dozen plays, and countless prose pieces, *The Secret Garden* has proven the hardiest.

The book, first published in serial form in 1910, has inspired artists, filmmakers, musicians, and dramatists. There have been illustrated editions, Broadway and West End musicals, movies, a statue in New York's Central Park, and a Japanese anime television series. For over a century, gardeners have been drawn into the story of Mary, Dickon, Colin, and the garden inside the locked door at Misselthwaite Manor.

If you have not yet read *The Secret Garden*, I hope that you will. It is a gardening book you will never forget, the first book that sparked my interest in making a garden. My garden. And in one of those strange quirks, Frances Hodgson Burnett and I share a birthday, November 24, though 108 years apart.

This book looks at the development of *The Secret Garden* and explores one facet of a complex individual and prolific writer, that is, Frances Hodgson Burnett as a gardener. Burnett herself will show the way. The book follows her through the places and plants of her life, before, during, and after *The Secret Garden*. It focuses on her three beloved gardens in England, America, and Bermuda. Since only the

English garden, now called Great Maytham Hall, continues to be cultivated on the scale of Burnett's gardening endeavors, you will find many photographs of its flowers and features.

The centerpiece of the book looks inside *The Secret Garden* and its particular brand of horticultural magic. A sampling of Burnett's other garden-related writings—at least those that I have discovered so far—are in the final section, "Outside *The Secret Garden*." These include a *Country Life* article about her garden in Kent, a narrative about a robin in her English rose garden, and a horticultural essay written during her final illness in 1924.

Like dedicated gardeners since Adam and Eve, Frances Hodgson Burnett passed a love of gardening to her offspring. Her only surviving son, Vivian, shared it in turn with his daughters, and so on. The family tree seems to have borne at least one avid gardener per generation. This book closes with an afterword by Burnett's great-great-granddaughter, Keri Wilt, gardener and writer. If you would like to tuck a few of Burnett's favorite flowers into your borders, you will also find an annotated list of plants she knew and grew.

A note on the use of names. When referring to the author of *The Secret Garden*, I will refer to her as Frances Hodgson Burnett, which she used as her professional name from the time she was married, or simply Burnett. I will take the liberty of calling her by her given name when she is a child and when she is at leisure.

Now let's find the key, unlock the door, and step into *The Secret Garden* and the gardening life of Frances Hodgson Burnett.

PART ONE

before THE SECRET GARDEN

Mary Lennox uncovers the hidden door to the garden, illustrated by
Charles Robinson for the first London edition of *The Secret Garden*.

THE
LOCKED
DOOR

ENGLAND & AMERICA
1849 – 1897

So long as one could not cross the threshold,
one could imagine all sorts of beautifulness
hidden by the walls too high to be looked over,
the little green door which was never unclosed.

—From *The One I Knew the Best of All* (1893), describing
a garden door from childhood

NEVER UNDERESTIMATE THE power of a garden to tell a story. In the case of *The Secret Garden*, Frances Hodgson Burnett recalled her feelings as a gardener and about a particular garden. It was an English garden that she had made and lost, her first real garden. With her always-active imagination and perennial search for material, she wove in people she had known: a gardener, a sick boy, men disabled in body and spirit. She also drew on the person she knew, or at least thought she knew, best of all—herself.

MANCHESTER, ENGLAND
(1849–1865)

She was not born a gardener. The future author of *The Secret Garden* did not take up serious gardening until she was almost fifty years old. Fortunately, the soil was prepared much earlier. And as bona fide fairy tales go, Frances Hodgson Burnett's life isn't bad. Hers is a riches-to-rags-to-riches story, set in the dark city and the pastoral countryside. There are heroes and villains, love and hate, intrigue and adventure.

She was born Frances Eliza Hodgson on the 24th of November 1849 to parents living in the Cheetham Hill neighborhood on the outskirts of Manchester. One might have described them as reasonably well-to-do. Her father, Edwin, was an ironmonger (or so he described his profession on the church registry the day of her baptism), but an ironmonger of a refined sort. His business offered

The illustration for the humble but fragrant violet in Frances's first alphabet book in an edition by Dean & Son.

elegant fixtures and fittings for homes of the burgeoning middle class in this, the Cottonopolis of industrial England, and it maintained his family in comparable style.

Frances was the middle child of five, balanced between two older brothers and two younger sisters. She had nurses and maidservants and every expectation of comfort. She had the frequent attentions of a grandmother who loved to read.

Grandmamma brought the plump, rosy-cheeked three-year-old to the local bookseller to select her first book. It was a rhyming alphabet of flowers with color illustrations that popped out from black backgrounds. Looking back, Burnett remembered learning that A stood for Apple-blossom, P for Poppy, and R for Rose. She called it the "Little Flower Book," though from her description it was probably *The Alphabet of Flowers*, first published in London in 1850. "Such lovely pictures! So like real flowers!" she wrote of it. "As one looked at each one of them there grew before one's eyes the whole garden that surrounded it—the very astral body of the beauty of it."

While teaching young Frances her letters, the alphabet book also taught a language of flowers, full of etiquette and upstanding morals. She felt that "the Violet stayed up all night, as it were, to be modest, that the Rose had invented her own sweetness." Here's one example, a lesson in sharing:

> *U unable to bring, of its*
> *own, any flower,*
> *Prayed V to lend one he might*
> *have, in his bower;*
> *V, like a kind brother, the*
> *VIOLET lent,*
> *Saying, "Humble it is, but*
> *prized for its scent."*

Is it any wonder that Burnett's adult prose was infused with floral references? Nor is it surprising that she sometimes veered into the Victorian language of flowers. Her ideas about flowers were built up from years in a proper English nursery and schoolroom.

Young Frances perched on the bookcase or *secretaire*, as she called it.

The first childhood garden that Burnett remembered was behind their comfortable home on St. Luke's Terrace, near the Anglican church in Cheetham Hill. Though a hedge was the only thing separating the rear of the property from the neighbor's pigsties, it was "the back garden of Eden" for Frances. This paradisal domain was lush with lilacs, rhododendrons, laburnums, viburnums, and small fruit trees. "There were roses in bloom, and a score of wonderful annuals, and bushes with gooseberries and red and white and black currants, and raspberries and strawberries," she later recalled, "and there was a mysterious and endless seeming alley of Sweetbriar, which smelt delicious when one touched the leaves and which sometimes had a marvellous development in the shape of red berries upon it." As in other Edens, sadly, the Hodgsons' tenure at St. Luke's Terrace was cut short.

In 1853, when her father died without warning, her mother donned both mourning garb and the mantle of the Hodgson business. Trade gradually diminished, and so did the family's prospects. As in Jane Austen's novels, the Hodgsons were forced to retrench on more than one occasion. Eliza Hodgson relocated her family several times in Greater Manchester, slipping stepwise down the social ladder with each move.

Mamma eventually settled the family in Islington Square in Salford. Burnett described it as a place for "widowed ladies with small incomes, and *un*widowed gentlemen with large families—people who, not having been used to cramped quarters, are glad to find houses of good size at a reduced rent." The surroundings were bleak and the air full of "smuts"—ash and soot from the coal-fired factories.

While in its better days Islington Square might have had at its heart a green park, only a paved area with a central lamppost remained. There was one brave bed of flowers in a neighbor's front garden, growing in stark contrast to what Burnett called the "ugliest, smokiest factory town to be found anywhere in all the North of England." Just outside the iron gates that marked the entrance to Islington Square was a warren of back alleys, and slum housing that Friedrich Engels dubbed "cattle-sheds for human beings."

Frances and her friends talk with one of the "street children," illustrated by Reginald Birch for *The One I Knew the Best of All*.

Young Frances was warned to avoid contact with children from the other side of the gates, an admonition that she furtively ignored. From these acquaintances, she learned the Lancashire dialect. She later employed her linguistic ear in writing the dialogue for many characters, including the broad Yorkshire of Martha, Dickon, and Susan Sowerby in *The Secret Garden*. Its heroine, Mary Lennox, was

23

similarly independent-minded and proud of her ability to speak "a bit o' Yorkshire."

Frances always loved a good story. When she was old enough to climb the shelves in her parents' library, she discovered Harriet Beecher Stowe's *Uncle Tom's Cabin*, another book laced with flowers and gardens. It caught her imagination and motivated the acquisition of a new doll named Topsy and the rechristening of another as Eva. The family bookcase also held bound volumes of *Blackwood's Edinburgh Magazine*, known for its romantic, historic, and gothic fiction. As an adult Burnett recalled vivid details of the magazine's serialized novels such as *The Scottish Chiefs* and *The Mysteries of Udolpho* written by Jane Porter and Ann Radcliffe, respectively. Charles Dickens, James Fenimore Cooper, Sir Walter Scott, and William Thackeray also held valued places in her pantheon of authors.

By now school-aged, Frances and her sisters attended the Select Seminary for Young Ladies and Gentlemen in Islington Square. While arithmetic was a trial, she excelled in reading and spelling. History was another of her strong subjects, both ancient and British, though only "up to the … Georges," where she found the romance ebbed away. She soon started inventing stories of her own, entertaining her classmates with elaborate narratives of thrills and romance whenever the schoolroom went unsupervised.

In her memoir, *The One I Knew the Best of All*, Burnett wrote that she "adored the stories in which people had parks or gardens, or lived in rustic cottages, or walked in forests, or across moors, or climbed 'blue hills.'" She gardened in her imagination, transforming the drab

Square in her mind's eye with fantasies of bluebells, harebells, roses, and an ornamental lake with swans. She was always lavish.

Another garden of her childhood imagination has a direct link to *The Secret Garden*. Behind a vacant mansion in the vicinity of Islington Square was a wall with a green-painted door, a door with a vague air of mystery. On hearing that the house was to be demolished, she opened the door and discovered a lost garden that bears an uncanny resemblance to Mary Lennox's in the novel. "At least it had been a Garden *once*," Burnett remembered, "and there were the high brick walls around it—and the little door so long unopened, and *once* there had been flowers and trees in it… though it was so long ago." In this abandoned garden room, she concocted a pretend scene: a rose-covered bower, swaths of flowers, avenues of beech, oak, and chestnut. The actual space was rubbish-strewn and choked with weeds. There was one exception, a tiny red flower blooming along the ground, like star-shaped cheerfulness. She thought it might be scarlet pimpernel.

Other realities could not be avoided. In 1865, Eliza Hodgson gave in to economic facts. She had been trying to run a fine furnishings business in a city careening under the Cotton Famine. It was a perfect storm for manufacturing: overproduction preceding a shrinking world market for cotton goods, then a precipitous drop in raw fiber from plantations in the war-torn American South. Manchester's main industry crashed. Mills and textile works closed. Vast numbers of people—labor and management—lost their jobs. Bankruptcies were rife. Demand for the luxury goods offered by the Hodgson business evaporated. The family packed up once more, this time for

25

Of her identification of scarlet pimpernel Burnett later mused, "It did not really matter whether [I] was quite right or not—[I] loved the name and hoped it was the real one."

a more radical move. They boarded a ship for a trans-Atlantic crossing and made their way to Knoxville, Tennessee, the home of Eliza's brother, William Boond.

EAST TENNESSEE
(1865-1873)

William had been effusive in his invitation to his sister. He promised her boys employment in his provisions business, where he sold everything from groceries and dyestuffs to nails and baling twine. As it turned out, Boond's commercial boom went bust when the American Civil War ended in 1865, just as the Hodgsons arrived. Uncle William did his best, arranging for one of his nephews to work at his rural grain mill and the other in his store on the corner of Gay and Union Streets in Knoxville. For Eliza and his three nieces, he offered a house—a ramshackle log cabin—in the village of New Market twenty-five miles away. At least it was a roof over their heads.

The words "practically starved" are often applied to this period in the family's history. The boys sent what money they could. Kind neighbors stopped in with extra food to help these genteel, impoverished Englishwomen transplanted to the Tennessee hills. Frances and her sisters started a local school, though their pupils tended to pay in eggs and meat.

Despite all these trials, Frances delighted in the landscape. The skies were vast and blue, and she was surrounded by forest and purple hills. Birds sang. Bees droned. She felt "not a stranger here,"

27

but a part of it. Her memories of these teenage years verge on the transcendental:

> To get up at sunrise and go out into the exquisite fresh-
> ness and scent of earth and leaves, to wander through
> the green aisles of tall, broad-leaved, dew-wet Indian
> corn, whose field sloped upward behind the house to
> the chestnut-tree which stood just outside the rail fence
> one climbed over on to the side of the hill, to climb the
> hill and wander into the woods where one gathered
> things, and sniffed the air like some little wild animal,
> to inhale the odor of warm pines and cedars and fresh
> damp mould, and pungent aromatic things in the tall
> "Sage grass."

She described herself as something of a dryad—a fairy that lives in a forest.

Language also had its allures. As in Manchester, Frances picked up local dialect and idioms. She pictured the shock of her English cousins if they could hear her "speak American" with phrases like "I guess" and "I reckon." Grown into a petite young woman with violet eyes and a laughing personality, she acquired the nickname "Fannie." It was always fun when Fannie was around. "What larks!" she liked to say of her various escapades.

While New Market had neither the romance of James Fenimore Cooper's Mohicans nor the grace of Southern living as she had visualized it, she took to the new social scene and captivated the locals. Or so they remembered once she was famous. The local doctor's

The young Frances Hodgson became the primary breadwinner for her family.

son, Swan Burnett—two years older than Frances and planning to study medicine—was smitten from the start by this laughing, vibrant English rose. There was romance, or at least flirtation with romance.

Despite these distractions, poverty had no appeal. "Shabbiness as a rule is depressing," noted Burnett in the draft of one story. With her brothers' financial contributions, the family moved to a slightly better house, albeit a tiny one. It perched atop a hill with vast views of the Appalachian ridges. Frances called their new address "Noah's Ark, Mount Ararat." She filled their home with bouquets of wildflowers she gathered, but she yearned for more. More beauty. More security.

The woodland edge enticed her. A thicket of sassafras, sumac, and dogwood opened onto a small clearing crowned by a natural

The flavorful fox grape (*Vitis labrusca*), illustrated here by Helen Sharp,
is likely the grape that paid for Frances Hodgson's postage.

roof of wild grapevines. Frances called the spot her Bower. She was inspired to write there, scribbling stories on odd bits of paper. In inclement weather, she retreated to a small, unheated attic room, her "Temple of the Muses," and wrote among the rafters. Her sisters Edith and Edwina acted as audience and cheerleaders.

Writing offered a way out. Her principal object was, as she put it, "remuneration." There were opportunities; monthly periodicals encouraged submissions from readers. But what of the money for proper stationery and postage? Wild grapes from the Bower supplied an answer. Gathered in quantity and sold at the local market by "Aunt Cynthy's girls," who lived at the bottom of the hill, wild grapes were transformed into paper and post, like the magic that her characters would later invoke in *The Secret Garden*.

In June 1868, *Godey's Lady's Book* published her story "Hearts and Diamonds" under the pseudonym "The Second." Another story followed in October. And thus, at nineteen years of age, her writing career began. More than a dabbler, she went to work, producing a regular output that continued for the rest of her life. She became a regular contributor to several magazines including *Scribner's Monthly* and *Harper's Bazaar*, soon publishing as Fannie E. Hodgson.

With regular checks arriving, Frances immediately outearned her brothers, and the Hodgsons moved into Knoxville proper in 1869. They rented a run-down but beloved brick house that the family christened "Vagabondia Castle." The back of the property dropped down to the Tennessee River, which still flows through the heart of the city. The two brothers and three sisters, now in their teens and twenties, hosted lively parties and musicales. Perhaps there was a modest garden. In a book written decades later, she hinted, "I have made gardens in queer places. [N]ot large gardens and not through spending much money. But still gardens."

The Vagabondia days were brief. Eliza Hodgson, "Dear Mamma," died in 1870, aged fifty-five. The siblings dispersed with wedding bells ringing. Her eldest brother, Henry, and both of her sisters married within eighteen months. Frances, still pursued by Swan Burnett, finally married him in September 1873, though only after taking a year and a half abroad in Manchester, London, and Paris to visit friends and relations.

WASHINGTON, D.C., AND BEYOND
(1874–1897)

Their son Lionel was born on 16 September 1874. Six months later the small Burnett family, accompanied by "Mammy Prissy," their nanny-cook-housekeeper, left Knoxville for Paris, where Swan studied ophthalmology. Her editor at *Peterson's* advanced money against the promise of regular story submissions. Still the family breadwinner and soon pregnant again, Frances continued to produce story after story and started on her first novel. She worked herself to exhaustion. To her sister Edith she wrote, "I want my chestnuts off a higher bough."

A second son, Vivian, arrived in April 1876. Frances was determined, driven by ambitions for herself, her sons, and for Swan. She underscored her drive by adopting a more professional byline. "I

The only known likeness of Swan Burnett or "Doro," as Frances called him when they were first married.

right Burnett with her sons, Vivian and Lionel.

never was called Fannie until I came to America & I don't like it," she insisted to her publisher. "It is too babyish for a woman & might mean anybody. So if you please 'Frances Hodgson Burnett' in future." She stuck to that throughout her career, despite changes to her marital status.

After returning from Paris, the Burnetts settled in Washington, D.C., where her husband set up his medical practice, and Frances continued to write. And write. Her debut novel, *That Lass o' Lowrie's,*

33

The American linden's fragrant flowers attract bees as well as writers.

was a bestseller in 1877. Her "Tuesday afternoons"—salons at her home on I Street—were considered excellent entertainment for Washingtonians of an artistic bent.

She doted on her boys and vice versa. They called her "Mammy," "Dearest," and, once they'd learned French, intermittently "Cherie." She continued to write. She wrote at home, sequestering herself in a room on the top floor of their house. The boys sometimes crept upstairs. "[Lionel] is lying on the floor on his back under the table at my feet now & has not stirred for about twenty minutes," she informed one editor. "That is what in literary houses we call 'being good' & is the condition on which he is allowed to stay with me." In this room of her own—fifty years before Virginia Woolf declared the need for one—Frances found a garden, at least a garden of sorts.

A pair of maple trees grew outside the windows of her third-floor writing den. Their branches touched the sills. Sparrows nested in them and sometimes perched on her window ledge. Many years later, she told a friend that she had "once lived in the top of a tree & shared the domestic life of bird families."

Trees also seemed to speak to her, and fragrance, always. As money flowed in, she bought the family a more fashionable house near Dupont Circle. She cherished the lindens on Massachusetts Avenue, especially in spring. Turning the corner from the Circle, it was "odorous with the perfume of sun-warmed... blossoms." For her, it remained a haunting memory.

She had published a dozen novels for grown-ups before serializing *Little Lord Fauntleroy* in *St. Nicholas Magazine* for children.

ELSIE LESLIE, as LITTLE LORD FAUNTLEROY
Copyright 1888, by Napoleon Sarony.
37 UNION SQR. N. Y.

Two years after the book's publication, Burnett adapted *Little Lord Fauntleroy* for the stage, here with Elsie Leslie who played the title role on Broadway.

opposite Vivian Burnett posing as the inspiration for Little Lord Fauntleroy, a fact he couldn't shake for the rest of his life.

The craze for dressing boys in "Fauntleroy suits" persisted, as demonstrated in a 1926 portrait of my mother, two of her sisters and her brother—with the clothes but without the curls.

Burnett (far right) among "Eminent Women" including Louisa May Alcott (center front) in a composite promotional piece created for the Travelers Insurance Company in 1884.

Inspired by her precocious son, Vivian, the story moved solidly into the adult market in 1886 when released in book form. *Fauntleroy* was an international phenomenon—more than one person has called it the Harry Potter of its day. Burnett became a superstar.

When Burnett was lunching at the home of the poet's brother and neighbor in Amherst, Massachusetts, Emily Dickinson sent her "a strange wonderful little poem lying on a bed of exquisite heartsease in a bowl." Samuel Clemens (aka Mark Twain) admired her writing and bought his daughter Clara a copy of *Little Lord Fauntleroy* that Christmas. Burnett was a friend of fellow Anglo-American novelist Henry James and author-editor Mary Mapes Dodge, best known for *Hans Brinker, or The Silver Skates*. Everyone knew her name.

Boston culture beckoned. Louisa May Alcott, already famous for *Little Women*, wrote to a mutual friend:

> Yes, I am reading "Lord Fauntleroy," I think it charming. I see Mrs. Burnett as often as I can, I went to a gay little party at her friend's home on New Year's Eve. [Mrs. Burnett] is rather better, but mends slowly, & needs years of rest for her overworked brain. What a pity we cannot buy a new head as we do our bonnets.

Fame and overwork had had their price. Health problems—periodic bouts of depression, back pain, neuralgia, and digestive issues—dogged Burnett throughout her life.

Frances, photographed in 1888, loved fashion and always sported the latest styles.

At about the time when her boys went to school, Frances packed her trunks and, for much of the time, lived away. There was more than one reason. She tried various clinics and spas for cures. Business often called her to New York and London. She dramatized many of her novels and advised on scripts during the ramp-up of stage productions. Copyright laws at the time did not protect foreign authors, so she shuttled back and forth across the Atlantic on steamships. Residing at a permanent address in Great Britain for publication dates and theatre openings provided some legal protections.

Her travels were not solo wanderings. She was accompanied by one of a handful of close female friends or by her sister Edith. (Their other sister, Edwina, had settled on a California ranch with her family). Besides Manhattan and London—and rare visits to Washington—Frances stayed in various places. She still loved Paris, especially for its fashion. She was a regular visitor to Worth, the premier dress designer. She adored Florence. She spent a summer at Hartford, Connecticut's wealthy literary colony, Nook Farm. She was a guest of Isabella Beecher Hooker, though it is unclear whether Hooker's half-sister and neighbor, Harriet Beecher Stowe, was in residence during those months. For the most part, Frances transplanted easily. Wherever she landed, she had a knack for making a home and filling it with interesting people.

She and her husband grew apart. It seems she had romantic entanglements—their extents somewhat hidden by the veil of Victorian discretion. She definitely struck up a relationship with an English doctor-turned-actor, Stephen Townesend, whom she had met through London theatre friends. Over time, he assumed various roles in her professional life—managing contracts, appearing in some of her plays, and occasionally coauthoring scripts. She took to calling him "Uncle Stephen" in letters to Lionel and Vivian.

The two boys sometimes joined her in one place or another—France, Italy, England. More often, she was a long-distance parent. Imagine, then, her guilt when Lionel was diagnosed with consumption. Frances swooped into Washington from England and whisked him off to several sanatoriums, finally to Paris. In a rented apartment, she hired a cook, servants, and a private nurse for Lionel. With the doctor, they all did their best for "le petit jeune Monsieur" in the final stage of tuberculosis.

Stephen joined her in Paris, helping to care for Lionel as he grew weaker and weaker. Lionel died in Paris on 7 December 1890. He was sixteen years old. They buried him at the Saint-Germain-l'Auxerrois cemetery. Underscoring the shifts in her marital life, Swan was in Washington with Vivian when Lionel died.

Adrift with grief after the funeral, Frances wandered listlessly through Europe with her friend Kitty Hall as a companion. Her sad letters arrived on the black-edged stationery that marked the period of mourning. A few months later on the Riviera, her spirits lifted. Everything seems possible again in spring.

In a letter addressed from the Grand Hotel des Anglais in San Remo, she told Vivian that she was working again in the warm, soft days. There were so many flowers. "At every second step one is met by people in the streets carrying baskets of violets & jonquils

A rare surviving image of an adolescent Lionel Burnett.

& hyacinths for sale. One can buy for ten cents a bunch of violets one would have to give two dollars for in England or America at this season." Everyone was wearing corsages of violets. The air in the whole town was heavy with their fragrance, intense and sweet. Violets reminded her of Lionel, but somehow the pain had gotten easier to bear. The raw wound was healing over. A deep scar would remain, always.

For some years she kept a residence in London, leasing number 63 Portland Place. It was a posh address, an elegant Georgian town-house in the City of Westminster. Parallel to Harley Street where the most exclusive medical practices still congregate, Portland Place is a wide, tree-shaded road. In 1895, returning from a visit to friends in Hampstead, she wrote, "Hampstead is really delightful. I should live there if it were only in Portland Place." She loved the house and expended significant resources to decorate and furnish it just so. She entertained. She went out. It could be hard to concentrate on work.

But work she must. Burnett's work enabled her lifestyle. As much as she earned—she was among the highest-paid writers of her day—she spent. She was generous, perhaps overly generous, with friends, family, and charitable causes. In a book given to a young neighbor, she wrote, "Nature never yet made a human hand without putting into it something to give." It was a sentiment she lived by.

Frances was also a woman of appetites for travel, clothes, food, and society. When Vivian, by this time a student at Harvard, complained of his indolence, she admonished him by holding up a mirror to herself:

> I have reasoned it out to myself long ago that by nature
> I am lazy. I believe if I allowed myself I should be always
> dreaming & never doing anything. Best being forced
> either to work or to own none of the graces and beauties
> of life. I have will power enough to compel myself to do
> things. Human beings can do anything they set their
> minds to—if they set them hard enough.

And work hard enough she did.

With all her activities, gardening was not yet among them. Just two blocks north of her front steps, Portland Place terminates

Crocuses blooming in the lawn on a heavenly spring day.

at the Crescent and Regent's Park. Frances enjoyed promenading there decked out in her finery—a fashionable gown, hat, gloves, and perhaps a parasol, depending on the weather. One April afternoon she got back to her writing desk and wrote to Vivian at his Harvard address. "Today is a heavenly Spring day," she related. The park "is adorable—with bursting buds & crocuses in the grass & a lovely haze over it all as if it were a kind of Indian Summer." She didn't know it at the time, but she was soon to have a place to call home with gardens and bursting buds of her own.

45

Mary Lennox fits the key into the door, from the first American edition of *The Secret Garden*, illustrated by M. L. (Maria Louise) Kirk.

TWO

FINDING THE KEY

MAYTHAM HALL, KENT
1898–1908

Next year my gardens will be resplendent.

—From a letter to Vivian, July 1898

SOMETIMES ONE LIFE change can trigger another. After Vivian graduated from Harvard in 1898, Frances and Swan divorced. That year she made another decision, this one of horticultural significance. She would sublet the house in London and move to the country. With her sister Edith, she started taking forays into rural areas within easy reach of London to look at real estate. On 28 February, she outlined her choice at length to Vivian:

> I wish you had been with us when we went into Kent a couple of weeks ago. I think I am going to take a place called Maytham Hall, Rolvenden. It is a charming place with a nicely timbered park and a beautiful old walled kitchen garden. The house is excellent—paneled square hall, library, billiard room, morning room, smoking room, drawing room & dining rooms, seventeen or eighteen bedrooms, stables, two entrance lodges to the park, and a square tower on the roof from which one can see the English Channel. We are only ten miles from the sea & the roads are perfect for bicycling. The views from the windows are very pretty. Can you believe that I can get such a place for *less than half* what I pay for this house— not to *mention* the fact that the taxes will be about half what one is assessed in town. Then one lives so much more cheaply for a score of reasons and—most important of all I can work so much better in the country. It is under two hours from town so one can have Saturday to Thursday house parties and can also run up to London for either business or pleasure when it is necessary.

Maytham Hall with its tower as Burnett knew it.

It would be a perfect place to write. She extended an invitation to Vivian, promising that she would save the tower bedroom with the view for him, and mentioning that Hastings, famed for its William-the-Conqueror–1066 battle, was just a bicycle ride away.

Kent, a wide county southeast of London, is still called the Garden of England. And no wonder. Its warm weather, fertile soils, and plentiful water have long made it one of the country's

49

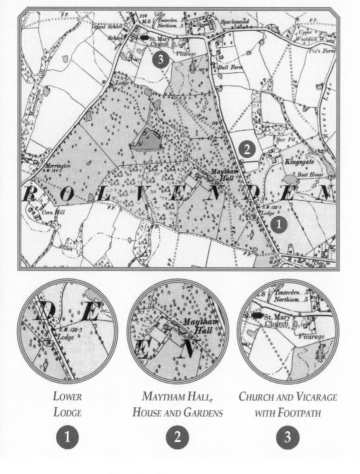

Maytham Hall and its locale, based on the Ordnance Survey map of 1899.

LOWER
LODGE
1

MAYTHAM HALL,
HOUSE AND GARDENS
2

CHURCH AND VICARAGE
WITH FOOTPATH
3

breadbaskets. Frances said she was "in the midst of the most picturesque county in England," and though one might not agree with the superlative, picturesque it is. Known for a heritage of hops and fruit-growing, it retained its rural and agricultural character. She loved the drives through Kent's country lanes. They wind through woodland and rolling hills, coastal marsh, and a stretch of the south coast that includes the White Cliffs of Dover. By the end of the

The expansive view of south Kent from the terrace at Great Maytham Hall, renamed after Burnett's tenure.

nineteenth century, the railroad had spread its tentacles into the county via the South Eastern Railway, making it easily accessible to Londoners like Burnett and her peers.

Maytham Hall was built in the mid-eighteenth century. Some hundred years later, it was topped with a third story sporting faux-Tudor detail. By the time Frances signed the lease, the interior had been extensively redone, in part to address damage from an 1893 fire. Its rooms were spacious, and, true to form, she set out to decorate. She and Edith camped out with the decorators while the work was underway. Her antique oak furniture suited the dining room with its three large windows that opened on to the park. The old billiard room became a red-walled family sitting room filled with bookcases, a worktable, and comfortable furniture arranged near the fireplace.

But the splendors of the house faded next to the property's real draw. When a journalist from *The Critic* asked how she chose Maytham Hall, Burnett responded, "Oh, the agent knew just about what I wanted, and when I came and that door was open, and I saw *this*, I decided at once." "This" was a wide stone terrace along the front or south side of the house. From it, over tennis and croquet grounds, she took in the wide lawn, tall trees, and the High Weald to the south. It seemed as if she presided over a kingdom that reached the horizon.

The grounds were extensive but had been somewhat neglected by the owner. There was a park—not a public park, but a private one, integral to any estate. A landed gentleman or lady would expect a long drive through their own personal landscape studded with stately trees and rolling lawns. Maytham Hall had its great oaks, horse-chestnuts, and beeches.

Frances began to garden as if making up for lost time. "The taking of Maytham Hall began a new era in her life, and introduced a new and consuming interest," wrote Vivian in *The Romantick Lady*, the biography of his mother he wrote after her death. "Here began what might be called her Pastoral period; here entered the Passionate Gardener." Frances told a friend that gardening was her new fad.

Maytham was just the place to indulge it. The formal grounds encompassed three acres of walled garden rooms, stretching south

The terrace at Maytham Hall planted with Burnett's roses.

Gooseberries and raspberries growing enthusiastically
in the walled kitchen garden at Maytham today.

opposite Burnett, always careful of her appearance in photographs,
chose to wear afternoon dress and a rose-bedecked picture hat in the garden for
her son Vivian's camera rather than her usual gardening attire.

from the main terrace. Flower borders flanked both sides of the walls.
Productive kitchen gardens grew in some of the buttressed brick garden rooms. Fruit trees espaliered against the brick were a feature. She
and Edith counted the many different kinds of fruits: apple, cherry,
and pear trees, gooseberries, and "currants of all shades." As soon as
she signed the lease, the gardener started sending up hampers of produce to Portland Place.

Gardeners are by nature a forward-looking lot, forever seeking the perfection that the next season might bring. Frances quickly took on the mantle of garden owner. Of course Maytham's gardens had run wild, they'd been neglected for so long. But not on her watch. Even before she took up residence she forecast, "Next year the gardens at Maytham will be twice as lovely as they can be this year."

She bonded with Bolton, the newly engaged head gardener, and described him to Vivian. "Bolton is a nice old thing who has been head gardener for twenty years at a large place and he is secretly filled with joy because I am 'a lady as loves flowers.'" It would be ten years before Burnett would sit down to write *The Secret Garden*. Without knowing it, she was absorbing material that would mold one of its characters, Ben Weatherstaff, gardener at Misselthwaite Manor.

That Frances loved flowers was no exaggeration on Bolton's part. She placed an initial order for over one hundred roses for the terrace and Rose Walk. She also gave Bolton leave to rehabilitate the flower gardens in a big way:

> I have 'allowed him' nearly three thousand new plants to
> fill the beds. He always touches his forelock & says 'I was
> a goin' to ask mum if you'd allow me so & so.' You see
> the plants put in this year will be in the beds—or in the
> greenhouses in the form of cuttings for next year & next
> & next &c.

Still, she tried to keep economy in mind. Plants didn't cost too much if one bought "by the dozen or by the hundred," she reasoned.

Burnett poured her relationship with Bolton into the character of Ben, the gardener in *The Secret Garden*, illustrated here by Nora S. Unwin.

The sundial became the centerpiece for the rose garden at Maytham Hall
and will reappear in *The Secret Garden*.

Bolton reassured her that gardeners he knew at nearby estates like
Hempstead Park and Rolvenden Old Park would give him divisions
of their plants too.

Within a few months, Bolton and his helpers had done the heavy
digging. They'd put in the roses and double dug the terrace beds and
the flower garden. While Frances often acted in a supervisory capacity,
she also got her hands dirty. On misty spring days, she knelt on a
rubber mat, tucking new plants in the prepared soil. Naturally, she

had put together special gardening attire—a hooded cape for chilly weather, a rubber apron for damp days, and "a red cotton frock, because it makes a bright bit of color in the landscape." She had fallen for gardening and fallen hard.

When the sun came out, it was time to shop for a hat to top off her garden costume. "One never knows what excitement is until one goes to shop in a country village," she reported. "When your carriage draws up before the drapers, you feel that you are a multimillionaire." And the bargains! In Rolvenden her garden hat cost four pence, three farthings. Once she'd trimmed it with silk and green ribbon—Frances was always handy with a needle—it was a hat that Liberty's would have priced at three guineas. Over fifty times more. Talk about London prices!

Always a quick study, she soaked up horticultural information from all sources. The gardeners taught her that the new vines that she'd asked them to plant near the walls were referred to as creepers. "In England nothing is called a 'vine' but the one which bears grapes." She read magazines, ordered books, and interviewed her gardening-inclined neighbors at length. By the following year, she boasted to her sister, "I shall have such worlds of things to tell you—learned things about flowers."

It was Maytham's old orchard that provided her ah-ha moment. Like much of the rest of the garden, it had thick brick walls with a patina of age. Opening the door in the wall and stepping through, she found a sundial that time seemed to have forgotten. The gnarled, lichen-covered fruit trees had long since stopped bearing. Bolton

59

The tiny Wittersham Road Station is still used by the Kent and East Sussex Railway for its seasonal heritage steam train.

urged her to replant. Let me replace those old trees, he urged. Why waste the space when, with new stock, it could be productive again in no time?

Frances saw something else. Magic. Maybe it reminded her of the humble bower in the Tennessee woods outside Mount Ararat, but this would be more. A garden. The ancient trees could be a living scaffold for a hanging garden of roses—columns of them, swags, and drapes. They would dapple the sunlight, shelter the birds, and create a fragrant retreat of yellow, white, pink, and crimson. She could change the space without losing its mystery. A curious little bird hopped out of the leaves and seemed to call its approval of her plan.

Almost before Frances had unpacked in the house, she started planting outside.

She loved to share her new garden with family and friends. Reading Burnett's note to journalist Mary Fanton, we picture two of her guests as they approach Maytham. "Dear Miss Fanton," she wrote on Maytham stationery:

> I felt sure you would achieve London. You know I said
> so. This is a line written in haste. I seldom go to London
> in the summer & should not be there before the 28th.
> I wonder if you and Miss Roof could come to us one
> Saturday and spend the weekend with us? The roses
> are not all out yet because the season has been cold but
> they are beginning to do their best, the darlings. Try
> to come and see them. We are easily reached. Here are
> your directions. Take the 4:50 train at Charing Cross to
> Robertsbridge. At Robertsbridge change to the little local
> train (which you will find waiting). It will trot along with
> you to Wittersham Road Station where the carriage will
> meet you & bring you to the Hall.

The carriage with its liveried staff ferried the guests along the park's three-quarter-mile drive, anchored at either end by Victorian gatehouses, the Upper and Lower Lodges, to be greeted at the Hall's front door.

Some weekends more than twenty or thirty people—agreeable, artistic people—descended on Maytham Hall, drawn by prospects of stimulating conversation, entertainment, and relaxation. Frances— called "Fluffy" by family and friends, though whether for her curly

61

Artist and Tennessee native Frank Richmond Kimbrough captured some of his fellow "Amuricans" in pencil at Maytham in 1901.

opposite American author Poultney Bigelow left this sketch of the festive atmosphere and "some of the Maytham Maniacs" in Burnett's guest book.

bangs, her rounded physique, her frilly wardrobe, or her personality is up for discussion—was something of a party girl. She told Edith that she would "turn Rolvenden into a Fluffy colony." When Americans arrived, she raised an American flag up the flagpole on the tower in salute.

She was an excellent hostess. There were strolls in the gardens, of course, and longer walks to show visitors grounds she found so

Some of the
MAYTHAM
MANIACs

under the
Spell of The

Honolulu Cake Walk.

I dont know this particular maniac but
he recalls your most grateful guest and
likewise something of a crazy crank

Poultney Bigelow

June 30.
1901

This newspaper illustration was captioned "Mrs. Burnett Reading a New Play to a Friend."

opposite The terrace at Maytham at present is planted with a vivid mix of floribunda and hybrid tea roses.

enchanting that Frances called them her "Fairy Wood." The athletically inclined engaged in wild croquet and tennis matches on the lawn with onlookers reclining on cushions strewn in the shade of trees. If guests wanted to relax, there were hammocks in a shady nook. She organized excursions to Canterbury or Hastings or Rye. Meals at Maytham were "huge laughing parties at breakfasts & lunches & dinners." For the servants it must have been like provisioning an army.

In the evenings after dinner, there was conversation—and cigarettes (Frances indulged). Dancing and cavorting followed,

accompanied by popular music rolling through her pianola. Sometimes she would read a passage from whatever new book she happened to be working on. A dramatic reading. Other times she would weave an impromptu gothic tale. One senses that in an alternate life, Burnett might have taken to the stage.

Some guests stayed for weeks rather than a weekend. A select few, being recognized as able hands, helped in the garden. Rosamund Campbell was an especially favored guest for her love of the spade. Frances enlisted one group of friends to hunt down greenflies infesting the rose garden. David Murray, a landscape painter, made himself popular by arranging a delivery of three hundred Laurette Messimy standard rosebushes.

Maytham was a welcome change from the social pressures of London. "I have artfully arranged things so that instead of seeing my friends in rooms crowded with people I see them in old gardens crowded with roses or in an old park crowded with trees," Frances purred in a self-satisfied letter to her editor at *Century Magazine*. Yet with all these distractions, she didn't forget her trade: mornings were reserved for writing. She went on, "Beautiful people lie on cushions on my lawn in the shade, but *I* am toiling."

When toiling, she preferred a pen to a pencil. The typewriter killed her imagination, and dictation—never. "I've tried," she once said to an interviewer, laughing, "but the mere sight of the person calmly sitting by, pen in hand, paralyzes me. It is too terrifying—like having one's picture taken, or being interviewed."

Her favorite place to work was the rose garden, sitting at her writing table on a rustic wood chair near the old sundial. There was a red Japanese umbrella to open if the sun became too bright. A robin she had befriended often twittered nearby. One day the robin surprised her by landing in the artificial roses on her sunhat. If it was very hot, Frances relocated to the dense shade of holly trees. In wet or cool weather, she sat by the leaded windows in her den where she could glance out onto her lovely terrace.

Things seemed to be going swimmingly when she made a major change. On 15 March 1900, the society column of London's *Morning Post* announced the nuptials of Mr. Stephen Townesend, the Inner

Temple, London, to Mrs. Frances Hodgson Burnett, of Maytham Hall, Rolvenden, Kent. Oh, Frances, what were you thinking?

This second marriage, particularly to a man eight years her junior, brought her unwelcomed notoriety. Reporters hounded her. One U.S. tabloid printed a full page of exaggeration with the headline, "The Amazing Marriage of Mrs. Hodgson Burnett, America's Great Woman Novelist, to Her Private Secretary, Young Enough to

The following text appears within the newspaper clipping image:

Love's Afternoon in the L
Little Lord Fauntleroy's Mann
The Amazing Marriage of Mrs. Hodgson Burnett, America's Great Woman Novelist, to Her Private Secretary, Young Enough to Be Her Son.

THE YOUNG SECRETARY.

This 25 March 1900 clipping from the *New York Journal and Advertiser* is one example of the sensational coverage of Burnett's second marriage.

Be Her Son." If the newspapers were scandalized, so it seems was Vivian, as the letters her son wrote to her during this time have vanished from an otherwise complete correspondence.

The marriage seemed doomed from the start. In February, Frances and a female companion had boarded a ship bound for the Mediterranean and disembarked in Genoa to meet Stephen for a quiet ceremony out of the public eye. First, they couldn't find him. After they managed to rendezvous and accomplish the ceremony, the weather turned rainy and cold. So much for an idyllic elopement on the Italian Riviera. At the Grand Hotel—a converted palazzo in the village of Pegli—she was forced to spend the honeymoon with her fur coat buttoned up to her neck and two hot water bottles to warm up her bed each night. If the wedding trip was a disaster, so was Stephen's behavior.

Townesend, while he could be endearing, had always been prone to rages and tantrums. He'd take an intense dislike to her friends. He'd shout and create scenes. It's puzzling why she married him, though he had harangued her to do it for some time. Marriage did not change him. Two months after the wedding, she wrote to Edith, "I am obliged to say that he scarcely seems sane half the time." It was a dreadful match, and within two years they were divorced. At least she had kept control of her money and the use of "Burnett" as her professional name.

With her life in turmoil, the garden was more than a distraction. It was her escape, her cure. To a journalist, she explained:

> To get down and dig in the warm earth—just to smell it—is to feel new strength; and the seeds and bulbs one plants revivify—they are so full of promise of life to come … Watch them grow. They have so much energy and so much imagination that they'll do beautiful things and make themselves beautiful in doing them.

Four years hence, Burnett would develop this theme into *The Secret Garden*. Frances felt that she belonged at Maytham Hall. While she didn't own it, it was hers—her real home. While she often dodged the worst of the winter months, she gloried in growth and change in her gardens across the arc of the year. Every season seemed to be lovelier than the last.

The tender green of the first spring leaves.

SPRING AT MAYTHAM

Spring is a thing which taunts one.

—From a letter to Edith, May 1899

F RANCES WAS IMPATIENT. Ever eager for the new growing season, she complained, "English weather is a thing to shake your fist at." Winter seemed reluctant to wane, recalcitrant even. Dampness and chill seeped through every gap in the Hall.

After winter seasons in London or on the Continent, Frances often came back to Maytham at the end of March, around Lady Day, the 25th of the month. She would find the house "a catacomb of cold." The ceilings were high, and the floors were flagged with black and white stone that seemed frozen. Most of the rooms had been closed up, as only the caretakers stayed in residence for the winter. While there was central heating, it took time to make a dent in the chill. Late storms—Frances called them "equinoctial gales"—howled

An illustration from *The English Flower Garden* (1900) gives
a sense of the snowdrops naturalized at Maytham Hall.

outside. It was misery. Her Tennessee relations would have said she
had cabin fever.

Then one day the sun would break out in such brightness that
everything surrounding Maytham Hall seemed to wake up at once.
Frost retreated. The trees in the park would start to soften with a
yellow-green haze of leaves easing out of winter buds. Something
stirs the blood at that first tender scrim of foliage, sheer as the foam
at the edge of a wave.

Maytham Hall's woodlands whitened with snowdrops, as if
someone had strewn white confetti by the armful across the forest

floor. Their small white flowers bounced and shivered in any breeze, shrugging off winter's coat. Typically called "common snowdrops" to distinguish them from more sophisticated varieties, they are far from common to pull off such a feat. They turned the woods into a land of make believe, and all before the ground thawed.

The flower beds were surveyed for signs of activity. She watched the perennials, the ones that had died back over the winter. "The herbaceous plants are my favorites," Frances once confessed, "for they come up year after year, and one learns to watch for them and welcome them like old friends." Day by day she watched them, their brown, dried crowns, trimmed neatly the previous autumn. One day there would be silence, the next some whispers of new growth. A week later they were up in force. Dear old friends.

And then more early bulbs—so many bulbs—accelerating from those first clumps of crocuses that opened their throats in the garden beds. Crocuses were joined by a procession of others across the park and gardens. Some years later when Burnett sat down with pen and paper to write *The Secret Garden*, she would immortalize Maytham's emerging bulbs as the "sharp little pale green points" that Mary Lennox first discovers at Misselthwaite Manor.

Spring brought migrating birds back to Maytham Hall's hundred-plus-acre park, piping like the church's organ. Nightingales reappeared sometime in April, and their crescendos filled May and June evenings. Frances had always been captivated by the liveliness of birds. As a child she had drawn them over and over in an old ledger book. The birds signaled spring at Maytham, and she reveled in it:

Like cuckoos calling, the wild primroses (*Primula vulgaris*) are a signal of spring's entrance into the English countryside.

left The little green points of snowdrops (*Galanthus nivalis*), spiking through leaf litter on the forest floor in late winter

You want to go out & walk through greening lanes & listen to skylarks & robins & thrushes & bullfinches fluting & trilling & nightingales waking the air & cuckoos crying Spring to the world. You want to go and lie on carpets & cushions of primroses & wild anemones & the earth is soaked with rain. I never dreamed that there could be so many primroses in the world as are here on every side of me.

The primroses! A wild English primrose is joy in floral form. The yellow flowers inject a burst of brightness into the lawns after

In *The Spring Cleaning* (1908), illustrated by Harrison Cady, Burnett conjured up fairies called Green Tuggers to strongly encourage the primroses to emerge.

the dull shades of winter. From a vantage point at her den windows, Frances took in a low, primrose-covered hillside that made her catch her breath. It was a splendor of primroses. They seemed to smile, or maybe she was doing the smiling.

Over time Frances tampered with nature, as gardeners have been known to do, transplanting many, many wild primroses into her rose garden. Roses are uninteresting in spring with thorny, skeletal canes. One of the few fond memories of her second husband was Stephen helping her dig, carry, and replant all the primroses among the roses. She was pleased with the effect; once complete, the garden was wreathed in scattered clumps for an early bloom each year. Her creation was a wild garden, part of the Arts and Crafts movement then in vogue and popularized by Anglo-Irish garden guru William Robinson.

In a matter of weeks, Maytham's primroses gave way to bluebells—wild bluebells—covering the fading yellow with fresh blue. She couldn't have planned it better herself. In the woods and on the hillside near the house, there was such profusion, such pure color. Their wafting scent was more than evocative. It was mesmerizing.

Frances often referred to bluebells as wild hyacinths. Whatever name you choose, bluebells are smaller than the stout flowers bred by the Dutch for centuries, though she planted Dutch hyacinths in her spring borders too. The wild bluebell (*Hyacinthoides non-scripta*) is native to England, calling the island home for as long as anyone remembers. An English bluebell wood on a spring day is transcendent, and Maytham's Fairy Wood was no exception.

Next came the larger bulbs. Frances loved tulips and hyacinths for their rainbow of colors in the flower beds. Daffodils seemed to fit in everywhere. She naturalized some of them in the lawn, echoing the wild daffodils that bloomed in the woods. Unlike in her more formal borders, she scattered the lawn bulbs in a random pattern to look like they had always grown there. She added masses of fragrant jonquils and the poet's daffodil with its bright white outer petals and tiny red-rimmed yellow corona. She didn't neglect the traditional daffodils—a word she seemed to apply to any type with a yellow trumpet—planting them in quantity. Requiring no more attention

Hyacinthus nonscriptus:
Blue Bell. Bell Bottle.

Douglas Isle of Man
June 10. 1894.

English bluebells are prized for their color, delicate habit, and scent, illustrated by Helen Sharp.

over An English bluebell wood is a dream.

Frances appreciated the reliable bloom and graceful outlines of the poet's daffodil (*Narcissus poeticus*).

than daisies in the pasture, the best thing about daffodils for Frances was their reliability.

Burnett's gardener was so pleased that he showed off the results to his own circle. "Bolton has been bringing rival gardeners in by the back gates in swarms," she reported to her editor, Richard Watson

Gilder. "He is a proud gardener & has attained a boastful chuckle." Frances glowed with pride. Always ready to try her hand at dialect, she recorded Bolton saying, "Tere aint no sich beds nit in Rolvenden, nit in Tenterden, nit in the whole county." To clarify she added, "'Nit' seems to be Kentish for 'neither.'"

Ornamental trees close to the house came into bloom. Some former Maytham owner, probably the Monypennys, had planted a collection—an arboretum of sorts—to adorn the views to and from the Hall. Frances was an appreciative audience, delighting in the hawthorns and the pink horse-chestnuts on the north lawn. The rosy candles of horse-chestnut flowers were a revelation.

In late April and throughout May, the flowering shrubs stepped forward. Massed azaleas and rhododendrons accented the slopes along Maytham's wide south lawn. Even the hedgerows came into bloom. Along the roads and between the fields around Rolvenden, generations of farmers had planted thick barriers of mixed shrubs to delineate fields and barricade animals. It was planting with purpose. The hedgerows grew into living fences that frothed with the flowers of hazel and wild hawthorn in spring.

At last, roses old and new swelled with green buds. Slowly, slowly the buds elbowed out into compound leaves. Frances couldn't wait to see them come into flower. Spring was the garden's prologue. "We are waiting with much excitement to see the blaze of beauty it will be in the summer," she told Edith.

Burgeoning roses on the terrace at Great Maytham Hall.

SUMMER AT MAYTHAM

The Rose Garden is sumptuous.

—From a letter to Edith, June 1900

THE BLAZE OF beauty was not long in coming. As summer unfurled, blue and white lupines punctuated the perennial borders along with clumps of scarlet Oriental poppies, bouncing on wiry stems. Lilies followed suit, adding height and drama. More than any other flower, though, roses dominated at Maytham Hall. They were the thread that pulled together the various walled garden rooms. Roses filled the generous terrace beds along the back of the house, overlooking the great lawn. They flanked the long path along the gardens so completely that Frances renamed it the Rose Walk and festooned its walls with climbing varieties.

Her favorite venue for roses was by far Maytham's sunny old orchard, the one that had so taken her fancy. It was enclosed by high brick walls on two sides and a tall hedge of laurel on a third. The

Frances can be excused for pride in this waterfall of roses trained into an old apple tree in her rose garden. (Her writing table and chair are just visible in the shade on the left.)

opposite Frances looks over the wall of her rose garden with its green door ajar.

back was edged by the towering trees and dark shadows of the Fairy Wood. Among the wizened fruit trees, Bolton and his staff planted climbing roses, tying them to the twisting, lichen-bearded trunks. As the canes shot up, the gardeners trained them into the framework of limbs, transforming the space into waterfalls of roses. This garden, a garden of her own invention, she would come to celebrate in *The Secret Garden*.

Just a year after she moved in, she felt her roses lent her bragging rights. And Bolton was as besotted with the summer garden

85

Lavish apricot trusses open on Champagne Moment, a floribunda rose at Great Maytham Hall.

left A pale yellow climbing rose lights up one of Great Maytham Hall's old brick walls.

as he had been with the garden in spring. A neighbor's head gardener told him that compared to the gardens of Lord Medway, the Earl of Cranbrook, and many more, "there were no such roses as [Maytham's] anywhere in the county." Who wouldn't be proud?

Frances was no idle dabbler. As well as absorbing knowledge from Bolton, her bookshelves started to fill with gardening books. *My Roses and How I Grew Them* was a favorite, a chatty how-to by children's author Helen Milman Crofton, a devoted amateur rose grower. For specifics on rose selection and care, she often consulted one of the volumes written by Anglican priest and gardener Samuel Reynolds Hole.

Speaking of clergy, her secret source of expertise on all things rose-related was the vicar. "As long as there are gardens and vicars in the British Empire, there will be fresh and useful information to be had about roses and their various virtues and shortcomings," Frances once exclaimed, "for the vicar is to the rose family what Boswell was to Johnson." Or perhaps Florence Nightingale would have been a better comparison. Whenever she ran into trouble with her roses—and roses are plagued with a plethora of pests and diseases—she "unburdened [her] troubles to a vicar." Invariably practical first aid was prescribed, packaged with sympathy and wisdom.

She learned the ways of roses. They are hungry plants, "greedy beyond almost any flowers," so she ensured that they were properly fed week by week and in the proper season. Knowing that her roses would flower more profusely if deadheaded regularly, she would walk out with her shears and "cut the roses every day to keep them blooming." One evening she cut about half a bushel.

Along the brick wall of the rose garden, she trained more climbing roses. One visitor remembered the wall "topped all its picturesque length with more roses that grew to an arrogant size and beauty out in the constant sunlight." Frances garlanded every arch and gateway into the garden with rambler roses in shades of crimson and pink, entwined with flowering vines—clematis and jasmine.

By 1900, she was sending regular baskets of cut roses to friends in London, sharing her floral wealth. Her letters from Kent—and later from Long Island—often mention garden flowers for delivery to her urban circle. Another of the books on Burnett's shelves, *Pot-pourri from a Surrey Garden* by Maria Theresa Earle, lets us in on the method. The cut roses soaked in pans of water overnight. The next morning Frances—or more likely the staff—dried them, rolled them tightly in newspapers, and packed them into a basket or box for the Maytham driver to bring to the station in time for an early London train.

Sometimes her promises to send roses backfired. Among her London acquaintances was Anglo-American painter George Henry Boughton. Frances had pledged a delivery of Maytham roses to his London studio for him to paint. In a tone of mock penitence, she was forced to write an apology:

> I had boasted—indecently boasted—of my roses, and flaunted them before you, and after you had paid them the compliment of asking that some might be sent to you to make immortal in a picture, I never sent them. The truth was that when I returned to Maytham I found they were suddenly developing mildew, which blurred all their glory. My head gardener says it was because of the "dryth" but I believe it was mere haughtiness at hearing you were going to paint them—or else it was a desire to lay me low because I had boasted.

Undaunted, Frances went on to extend an invitation to Boughton and his wife. Come to Maytham, she urged, adding that he

Roses arch over a door at Great Maytham Hall
in homage to its most famous tenant.

Frances at her writing table in the rose garden.

surely would want to paint her quaint and picturesque rose garden among the old orchard trees *en plein air*.

Frances aspired to hosting a brilliant summer each year at Maytham, with "such people & such flowers." She planned extravaganzas, capitalizing on her role as lady of the manor. During more than one summer she put on village fêtes—primarily for the locals—inviting all the children and mothers in the area to come spend a day in Maytham's park and on its lawn. On one such occasion, she hired a Punch & Judy show and organized races. The lawn-mowing donkey was enlisted, adorned with ribbons for donkey rides. The justice of the peace "carried about tea in a watering pot like an angel" and the Sunday school children "dispensed blocks of cake after the manner of seraphim." It was a heavenly day.

Another summer she staged a match on the village cricket grounds—Maytham Hall against Rolvenden. Every event was an excuse to fill the house to the brim with her own set. There could never be enough friends or enough roses.

More than anything else at Maytham, the rose garden was her creation. It held her attention—one might say her devotion—for the years that she lived there. It was her place of work, her outdoor sanctuary, and the place that she most often wrote about to farflung friends and family:

> How you would love the old trees and the old walls and
> the quiet of it—the seclusion—the sense of being near
> nothing but birds—and of hearing nothing but the lit-
> tle carols or twitters or calls, mingled with the sounds
> of leaves and bees. It seems to me that there could be
> nowhere in the world a sweeter place to write.

She savored it. Flutter. Chirp. Rustle. Buzz. Summer seems to stretch on at Maytham Hall, but neither sweetness nor summer lasts forever.

Autumn casts its long shadows in Maytham's park.

below While there seem to be no images of Maytham Hall's gardeners, this period photograph from Kew provides a window on the work of bulb planting.

AUTUMN AT MAYTHAM

I cannot write among roses much longer.

—From a letter to Vivian, September 1904

A UTUMN INSINUATES ITSELF slowly into summer at Maytham Hall. The quality of light changes, shifting to an angled elegance that elongates the shadow and backlights the bloom. Frances would hold on to her practice of writing outdoors for as long as possible. "The golden days go on & on as I never saw them in England before." The endless hours of an English summer day shrink little by little. Crispness infiltrates the summer warmth, a subtle shift. On a late September day, she wrote to Vivian from her favorite rustic chair under the rose-embowered fruit trees, "This place is so good for work. Nothing is like the Rose-garden. I have been writing there for some time & I could almost weep because the air is just a little autumny." But one can't ignore the season's accelerating pace for long.

Old brick walls complement Maytham's autumn foliage display.

The fairy tree at Maytham—probably coppiced for wattle poles as a sapling—grew into a destination and venue for Burnett's storytelling.

opposite Moss on the buttress roots of one of Maytham's beeches seems to invite fairy folk.

With autumn comes a new round of work in Maytham's gardens. Bulb orders start to arrive in crates and need to be planted promptly. One year she reported to Edith that an order of eight hundred had just landed on her doorstep—larger bulbs like narcissus, tulips, and hyacinths, tiny ones like snowdrops, plus anemones and crocuses,

that are technically corms. A thousand-and-one more were expected soon. "Darling Bolton" and his staff must have been kept very busy putting them all in the ground.

Leaves are infused with new colors, sometimes vivid, sometimes muted. They provide Barrett, the housekeeper, with decorations for the tables. In the borders the dahlias are still prolific. Frances favored cactus dahlias. They light up her garden with starbursts of spiky color until frost. Their doubled ray petals curve back on themselves like tiny, improbable paper straws. As cut flowers in the house, the blooms are just as enchanting.

In the park leaves waft down, surely the jurisdiction of fairies. Tree structures are unveiled, branchlet to branch to limb, making connections like the plot in a story. The differences in bark become apparent. Frances prized one tree in particular, her "fairy tree," for

97

its five huge trunks emerging from a single massive base. She often escorted her guests to this arboreal marvel, using its pillared form as a backdrop to tell one of her stories. Friends consider a leaf from the fairy tree a prized souvenir of Maytham, promising its possessors a swift return visit.

Each November, the sweet chestnuts ripen and fall in a seasonal bounty. "Guess what!" Frances exclaimed in a letter to her sister during her first year at Maytham. "Chestnuts! My wildest dreams

With chestnuts like these, Burnett realized "wildest dreams" of abundant country life.

opposite
Maytham's chestnut tree still bears nuts.

are realized." Picking them was a treat, especially with friends. If a basket wasn't at hand, they would fill their hats. "You can't stop," she explained. "The moment you stand up you see a dozen beautiful fat brown, glossy things shining in the leaves & you can't pass them." It is addictive, if exhausting. Roasted chestnuts are their just reward.

Even with winter approaching, there is still real work to be done in the garden. The roses need winter protection. Beds call for digging over. Frances confided to Edith that she and her friend Rosamund

99

had "dug & developed tendencies such as are not usual with beauteous & fragile females." Never missing a chance for drama, she continued, "It may cause you a slight shock to learn that the one object of our united existences at this time is—Manure." Yes, manure.

Lest we think that Maytham's gardeners did all the heavy lifting, it seems that Frances and Rosamund were obsessed with manure. "We dig it into the earth about rose roots, we spread it—we weep because we have not enough of it & the farmers will not sell it." As a soil conditioner, well-rotted animal manure continues to be prized. It improves the structure and gently boosts the fertility. Burnett once referred to Maytham's soil as mellow, no doubt aided by her efforts with garden fork and spade.

As well as digging in the borders, Frances was forever improving the grounds of Maytham Hall on a larger scale, both putting in and taking out. A rustic bridge allowed new access to the park. Getting rid of hedges softened some of the boundaries of her garden. She enhanced views from inside the house by editing plants in front of selected windows. At her direction the gardeners cut new arches into the tall laurels and added trellis-covered entrances on the Rose Terrace. Until the day she left, she was always on the lookout for ways to make her garden better, despite the fact that she was only a tenant.

Burnett wrote *The Secret Garden* between 1908 and 1910 after a striking change of venue. In 1907, the owner of Maytham Hall decided to sell it, and Frances reluctantly let the opportunity pass by. Vivian, settled in New York, had convinced his mother to move back to America.

Frances would have loved the new borders in the walled gardens at Great Maytham Hall, including this mixed planting with fragrant Rhapsody in Blue roses.

She saw her beloved Maytham Hall again just before the sale of her furnishings. She had decided to have them auctioned, rather than shipping them across the Atlantic. Maytham was so radiant on that October day that she could hardly endure it. She moaned in a letter to Edith:

> Oh the great stately velvet fields of lawn—dropping into
> the park & melting into the landscape—the great trees—
> the green terraces—the massed flower beds—the beauty

The new owners of Maytham Hall redid the gardens extensively after
Burnett's tenure, as seen in a photograph taken by a member of the
Garden Club of America in 1929.

of it all lying golden in the late afternoon sun! The quiet
& dignity, the air of having been there always! That place
belongs to me—It is the only place I ever felt was *home...*
real home.

In a way, it was living at Maytham that had meant England to
her. She felt that her roots were being torn out of the ground. But as
much as she had loved Maytham, there was no going back. And, if
she had stayed, *The Secret Garden* might never have been written.

Maytham Hall was soon redone in the Classical Revival style
sometimes referred to as "Wrenaissance" after Christopher Wren, the
famous designer of St. Paul's Cathedral in London. The new owner
employed architect Edwin Lutyens—whether his partner, garden
designer Gertrude Jekyll, participated in the redesign is up for discussion. Some of the old brick walls with their enticing doors remain,
and there is still a lovely garden at Great Maytham Hall (the word
"Great" was appended after the redo). Now, more than a century after
her last season at Maytham, only a few of her original plants are still
alive; one, Frances's favorite rose, the wichuraiana in her rose garden,
still puts on a valiant show every year. But the spirit of Maytham's
gardens remains true to *The Secret Garden* and its author.

Great Maytham Hall today, with gardens tended for its residents and in honor of *The Secret Garden*.

PART TWO

inside THE SECRET GARDEN

Mary steps through the green door, illustrated by J. Scott Williams for the serialized launch of *The Secret Garden* in *American Magazine*.

THREE

A GARDENER'S GUIDE TO *THE SECRET GARDEN*

MISSELTHWAITE MANOR, YORKSHIRE

In the hidden garden—which I adore—many
strange and wonderful [and] quite natural
human things happen. Oh, I know quite well
that it is one of my best finds.

—From a letter to her English publisher, William
Heinemann, describing *The Secret Garden*, October 1910

T*HE SECRET GARDEN* opens in India. The British Crown rule of India—the Raj—stretched from 1858 during Queen Victoria's reign until after World War II. Frances had never traveled to India, but in her day the subcontinent had captured the imagination of Britons and the English-speaking world. The Indian culture had such spice and tropical color and heat compared to England's green and pleasant land. Rudyard Kipling, Burnett's contemporary, was publishing novels like *Kim* and *The Jungle Book*. In English gardens, designers were incorporating Mughal-influenced features—mosaics and water rills—into their elaborate plans. Burnett included India in eight of her novels besides *The Secret Garden*.

Nowadays we recognize the precarious gulfs that the Raj widened between race and class. Burnett underscored those gulfs in the dialogue she gave to her characters. In *The Secret Garden*, she also brought out the contrasts in her descriptions of climate, gardening, and, to a lesser extent, society in general.

Mary Lennox, the heroine, is the ten-year-old daughter of a busy British government official in India and an elegant but aloof mother. Mary is no one's idea of an appealing child. Pulling no punches, Burnett's narrator describes her straight off as "the most disagreeable-looking child ever seen" and "as tyrannical and selfish a little pig as ever lived." She was sickly and cross. Her sallow skin was as yellow as a plant starved for light. Small wonder her care was left to an ayah. Mary occasionally amused herself in the garden outside their bungalow, arranging the sandy soil into pretend flower beds stuck

An illustration of "Mary, Mary quite contrary" by M. L. Kirk, not for *The Secret Garden* but for a project that Vivian undertook—a periodical for the juvenile market— eventually published as *The Children's Book* (1915).

Loranthaceae Mistletoe 7

Mistletoe, from which the names "Misselthwaite" and "Missel Moor" derive,
illustrated by Helen Sharp.

with hibiscus blossoms. But usually it was too hot, and she was too ill and too ill-tempered.

As in many fairy tales—think Snow White or Little Red Riding Hood—the parents are taken out of the picture at the start. A cholera outbreak leaves Mary orphaned. She is temporarily placed with a clergyman and his wife and their five children. Noticing that she likes to make pretend gardens outdoors, the children taunt her with a nickname borrowed from Mother Goose:

> *Mistress Mary, quite contrary,*
> *How does your garden grow?*
> *With silver bells, and cockle shells,*
> *And marigolds all in a row.*

Needless to say, Mistress Mary earns her contrary nickname. In a telling scene, one of the children, seven-year-old Basil, suggests that she put a heap of stones in the center and pretend it's a rockery—an alpine garden. Mary's immediate retort? "Go away! I don't want boys. Go away!" She doesn't stay with the foster family for long.

Under the supervision of an officer's wife, the orphaned girl makes the long ocean voyage from India to England and to her new guardian. Her next phase is set. She is to be the ward of her widowed uncle, Archibald Craven, and reside on his vast Yorkshire estate.

Burnett introduces us to the setting of Misselthwaite Manor during Mary's long rail journey from London to the north. She is under the charge of Mrs. Medlock, Mr. Craven's stern housekeeper, who grudgingly relates a description of Mary's soon-to-be home. It is vast. The house, we are told, is six hundred years old, with nearly one hundred rooms, mostly unused, furnished with fine furniture and paintings. "There's a big park round it and gardens," Medlock adds, "and trees with branches trailing to the ground—some of them." With this first mention of Misselthwaite's fictional landscape, one can already see the parallels with the real landscape of Maytham Hall.

Different from Maytham is the novel's geographic locale. Rather than the rolling Kentish countryside, Misselthwaite Manor is set on the edge of Missel Moor, a fictional if realistic Yorkshire wild area. As an aside, "Missel" is a variant spelling for "mistle," as in mistletoe, the white-berried plant beloved for holiday decorations back to Druidic days. The high altar at York Minster is decorated with mistletoe each Christmas Eve, as it has been for centuries. Mistletoe can still be found growing wild in Yorkshire, though it is more common elsewhere in England.

Mary and Medlock, riding in the manor's carriage for the last leg of the journey, cross the moor at night. Rain drums. The carriage creaks and rocks through the darkness of a winter night. Ten-year-old Mary—perceptive if peevish—imagines the moor as the sea, but Medlock sets her straight. "It's just miles and miles and miles of wild land that nothing grows on but heather and gorse and broom, and nothing lives on but wild ponies and sheep." Mary simply didn't like it.

The light from the manor's lodge is a beacon across the dark moor. After passing the lodge, there were "still two miles of avenue

On first seeing the Yorkshire moors, Mary finds them
bleak, illustrated by Nora S. Unwin.

to drive through and the trees (which nearly met overhead) made it seem as if they were driving through a long dark vault." Burnett could have been describing Maytham's long park drive and ancient trees. Misselthwaite Manor itself seems dull and ugly, and Mary is dull and ugly and lonely. But spring awaited her—her first English spring— and what a spring it would be.

Gradually getting to know the house and its staff, Mary finds that mysteries abound at Misselthwaite. Uncle Archibald is a hunchback, away at present as is his habit, reclusive when at home. There is the dead wife, never spoken of. There are shut up rooms to explore. There are strange echoes—the wind "wuthering" (echoes of

115

Mary Lennox's robin, illustrated by Graham Rust.

left The winter gardens at Misselthwaite Manor seem dreary to Mary, illustrated by Charles Robinson.

Emily Brontë) and something that sounds like crying in the corridor. But best of all there is the story of a locked, forbidden garden with buried key and concealed door somewhere on the vast grounds of Misselthwaite Park.

Martha Sowerby, the cheeky, good-natured young housemaid, first mentions the secret garden, locked ten years before when Mr.

Craven's wife suddenly died. Martha is a good storyteller and distracts her new charge with stories of her own parents and her eleven little brothers and sisters, playing in their cottage garden and on the moor. Key to the book's plot will be Martha's brother, Dickon, who charms fauna and flora alike, and their mother, Susan Sowerby, the fairy godmother of the story. "Mother" takes Mary under her wing, though she remains offstage for much of the book.

Mary Lennox had arrived at Misselthwaite at the end of winter. The flower beds are empty. The fountain is shut off. The gardens are stiff, divided into walled outdoor rooms and connected by walkways. There are lawns and shrubberies. Some shrubs have been topiaried—Burnett describes them as "evergreens clipped into strange shapes"—but even those have slim appeal. In the kitchen gardens there are only winter vegetables and stark branches of fruit trees "trained flat against the wall" that seem contorted in an unnatural way. Mary isn't impressed. A courtyard clock chimes the hours, but time drags. Still, she befriends a gruff old gardener, Ben Weatherstaff, and perhaps most important of all, a robin befriends her.

The robin is the key. The robin finds a key, unearthing it at Mary's feet. And, by alighting on the ivy-curtained brick wall, it shows the way to a hidden door. Mary turns the key in the lock and opens the door slowly—slowly. Then slipping in and shutting it behind her, she looks around "breathing quite fast with excitement, and wonder, and delight."

She is inside the secret garden. Reader, you are there with her.

Mary sees the magic in her first look at the secret garden, illustrated by Inga Moore.

SPRING AT MISSELTHWAITE

But she was *inside* the wonderful garden and
she could come through the door under the
ivy any time and she felt as if she had found a
world all her own.

—*The Secret Garden*

THE SECRET GARDEN is revealed scene by scene through Mary's eyes. Only the robin, "who had flown to his treetop," accompanies her. "It was the sweetest most mysterious-looking place any one could imagine," the narrator tell us. Mary sees stone seats in evergreen alcoves and tall moss-covered urns—formal elements softened by age. The remains of grassy paths meander here and there. The garden's high walls are thick with leafless stems of climbing roses. Frances Hodgson Burnett infused her nostalgia for Maytham's rose garden into the atmosphere of the abandoned garden:

[O]ne of the things which made the place look strangest and loveliest was that climbing roses had run all over [the trees] and swung down long tendrils which made light swaying curtains, and here and there they had caught at each other or at a far-reaching branch and had crept from one tree to another and made lovely bridges of themselves. [T]heir thin gray or brown branches and sprays looked like a sort of hazy mantle spreading over everything, walls, and trees, and even brown grass, where they had fallen from their fastenings and run along the ground. It was this hazy tangle from tree to tree which made it all look so mysterious. Mary had thought it must be different from other gardens which had not been left all by themselves so long; and indeed it was different from any other place she had ever seen in her life.

Now it was to be hers, her own.

If you have ever stepped into a garden and felt a shiver of something—recognition? awe?—you have had your own secret garden moment. Nature and a gardener have conspired to make a place that resonates at the same harmonic frequency as your spirit. A mystery. Some combination of light, color, plant, and place causes it, like the golden mean employed by ancient architects. It is an effect to which every gardener aspires.

Mary is uneasy. Is the secret garden dead? Ten years is a long time to be neglected. The grass is brown, the rose plants look gray and brittle—something that never happened in India. But then she notices "sharp little pale green points" sticking out of the earth. "Yes, they are tiny growing things," she whispers to herself, "and they *might*

Mary clears around the "sharp little pale green points," illustrated by Nora S. Unwin.

be crocuses or snowdrops or daffodils." She starts to clear around them with a pointed piece of wood, by instinct wanting to give them more room to breathe.

Back in her room, she can't stop thinking about the garden. She is struck with a desire to see all the things that will grow in England, plant lust being common to most gardeners, new or old. "I wish—I wish I had a little spade," she tells Martha that afternoon. Worried that she will give away her secret, Mary quickly adds that she would like to make a little garden *somewhere*.

For the acquisition of the spade, Martha promises to employ her brother, Dickon. Mary sends along a written request with some money on Martha's next day off so that he can buy it in the village. "In the shop at Thwaite they sell packages o' flower-seeds for a penny each, and our Dickon he knows which is th' prettiest ones an' how to make 'em grow," Martha informs Mary in her broad Yorkshire. "Our Dickon can make a flower grow out of a brick walk. Mother says he just whispers things out o' th' ground."

Like the Greek god Pan, Dickon is at home in nature. Frances once referred to him as a sort of faun, and in the book, he is described as "a sort of wood fairy," red-cheeked and blue-eyed. He is slightly older than Mary—about twelve. In Dickon, Burnett created a character to embody her own connection with the animal world. She was convinced that in past incarnations she had been animals, especially birds. "I am such friends with them and I understand them so and they are so sure of it and are such friends with me," she had once said. And so it is with Dickon Sowerby.

Mary finds Dickon playing his pipe under a tree in the park, illustrated by Charles Robinson.

Mary first comes upon Dickon in person sitting under a tree in the woods adjoining Misselthwaite's gardens. He is playing his wooden pipe. Wild creatures are keeping him company. A crow named Soot. Captain the fox cub. Dickon unwraps a package for Mary. There is a miniature spade, plus a small rake, a garden fork, a hoe, a trowel, and some packets of flower seeds.

After a long conversation about flowers and growing things, Mary decides to share her secret with Dickon, sneaking him through the ivy-hidden door. His reaction doesn't disappoint. "Eh!" he gasps

123

Mary and Dickon discuss their garden plans surrounded by Dickon's rescued animals, illustrated by M. L. Kirk.

in an almost whisper. "It is a queer, pretty place! It's like as if a body was in a dream." Frances had gauged her friends' reactions to Maytham's rose garden in much the same way.

Over the weeks that follow, Mary and Dickon work in the garden—pruning, weeding, and avoiding detection. He teaches her about gardening. Perennials like lily-of-the-valley need to be divided.

Biennials require patience, growing green one year in order to bloom the next. Dickon reassures Mary that most of the roses are "wick," that is, very much alive. They make an unusual pair: a poor but much-loved boy in tune with the natural world and a stunted rich girl who grew up without affection.

Dickon is Mary's teacher at Misselthwaite in the same way that Frances's friends—and vicars—at Maytham had been generous with gardening lessons and advice. To make plants thrive, Dickon knows that one must "be friends with 'em for sure." Like his tame animal friends, garden plants need attention. "If they're thirsty give 'em a drink and if they're hungry give 'em a bit o' food." It's good advice for any gardener. Mary absorbs his lessons like a thirsty plant.

The two children decide to cultivate a different sort of garden. Unlike Misselthwaite's formal borders—tended by head gardener Mr. Roach and his staff—theirs will be a tad untamed. "I wouldn't want to make it look like a gardener's garden, all clipped an' spick an' span, would you?" Dickon asks. "It's nicer like this with things runnin' wild, an' swingin' an' catchin' hold of each other." Mary agrees. "It wouldn't seem like a secret garden if it was tidy." Like the rose garden at Maytham Hall, the secret garden is to be in the spirit of the Arts and Crafts movement.

With her new interest and activities, Mary's disposition improves as does her appetite. Then reality intervenes. Archibald Craven comes home to roost, and so does Mary's guilty conscience. In a tense interview with her uncle, she reverts into a plain fretful child, worried that he will ban her from the outdoors in general or the secret garden in particular. But he provides a chance opening when he asks if there is anything she wants. He meant a toy or a book.

Omitting the particular space she has in mind, Mary asks her uncle if she might have "a bit of earth [t]o plant seeds in—to make things grow—to make them come alive." Archibald Craven is stunned, reminded of Lilias, his dear wife, who had also loved to garden. "When you see a bit of earth you want[,] take it, child, and make it come alive," he responds, full of emotion. That was all Mary needed to hear. Craven leaves the next day for yet another tour of the Continent, and the secret garden is hers.

Permission, though, is followed by punishment in the form of steady rain, which douses her hopes for working in the garden. "The rain is as contrary as I ever was," Mary laments. One is reminded of Maytham's "equinoctial gales." Mary resents being kept indoors but entertains herself with illicit explorations of the unused wings of the house. In one room she discovers paintings, most notably a portrait of a little girl with a green parrot. In another she finds a pillow that houses an adorable family of mice.

Burnett had a flair for inhabiting the mind of a character, including a bored, curious child wandering around a manor house on a rainy day. In one of Misselthwaite's uninhabited rooms, a glass-fronted cabinet reveals a collection of little ivory elephants. Mary is intrigued with them, just as Frances had been during a stay in Switzerland ten years before she wrote the book. On Lake Geneva in 1897, she had acquired miniature ivory elephants from a charming shop in Montreux. She reported to Vivian that her smallest, the baby,

Mary approaches her uncle to ask for her "bit of earth," illustrated by Nora S. Unwin.

In the dark of night, Mary discovers her cousin, Colin Craven, in his sickroom, illustrated by M. L. Kirk.

opposite On a rainy day at Misselthwaite, Mary finds a collection of ivory elephants just like the ones that Frances had bought, illustrated by Graham Rust.

was about the size of a five-cent coin. "I have eight now," she admitted. "If I buy them one at a time I shall not feel the shock. I want a herd." She gave her herd a permanent place in *The Secret Garden*.

One night, Mary's explorations yield a discovery more critical than mouse families and miniature pachyderms. She learns the source of the cries in the corridor: her cousin Colin.

Her cousin! Yes, Colin had been born when his mother—Uncle Archie's wife—died. He is a shut-in, a chronic, complaining invalid whose spoiled self rivals Mary's. The staff is at his mercy. During his father's frequent absences, he is literally lord of the manor. Mary calls him young rajah. Mary's stories of India soothe Colin. Eventually she

129

trusts him enough to introduce him first to Dickon and finally to the secret garden.

Spring comes slowly in Yorkshire, as slowly as it had come at Maytham Hall, but is much anticipated. The moor seems to hold its breath. Then one day the world changes—sun, sky, air—shifting so suddenly that "something Magic" must have happened. "It's warm—warm!" Mary cries. "It will make the green points push up and up and up, and it will make the bulbs and roots work and struggle with all their might under the earth." She breathes in gulps of the air from the now-beloved moor.

Bulbs open. Crocuses don colors so tender that Mary kisses them. "You never kiss a person in that way," she sighs. "Flowers are so different." The birds of Misselthwaite Manor flute new pitches, just as they had at Maytham Hall. Leaves on trees open just enough to tinge the world, a green luster.

Mary runs into the room of her still bedridden cousin and throws open his windows. "Things are crowding up out of the earth," she trumpets:

> And there are flowers uncurling and buds on everything and the green veil has covered nearly all the gray and the birds are in such a hurry about their nests for fear they may be too late that some of them are even fighting for places in the secret garden. And the rosebushes look as wick as wick can be, and there are primroses in the lanes and woods, and the seeds we planted are up, and Dickon has brought the fox and the crow and the squirrels and a new-born lamb.

Mary opens Colin's bedroom window to share the arrival of spring, illustrated by Charles Robinson.

Colin is captivated. He orders the head gardener to his room and informs a bemused Mr. Roach that Dickon and Mary will conduct him out of doors in his wheelchair. Roach is to keep the staff away. Secretly relieved, Roach laughs to himself. He'd worried that the young master might demand to have all the oaks in the park removed or the like. Burnett often gives glimpses into the attitudes of the "downstairs" staff.

As the spring unfolds its finery, Colin now joins his cousin Mary and Dickon in the secret garden on any day that the weather permits.

Poppies, larkspur, and roses surround Mary, Colin, and Dickon
in the secret garden, illustrated by Charles Robinson.

SUMMER AT MISSELTHWAITE

And the roses—the roses!

—*The Secret Garden*

THE SECRET GARDEN is a story about transformation, about second chances and changes so astonishing they might be called miracles. As the growing season proceeds, the focus of the story shifts from Mary to Colin. On first reading the book, Colin Craven might seem a thief, hijacking the plot from its rightful protagonist. Knowing what we do now about the author, we can attribute the switch to her tender memories of her older son, gone for almost a decade when she wrote the book. When Frances Hodgson Burnett brings Colin into the secret garden, she seems to rewrite the ending of Lionel's story.

Spring turns to summer. Seeds that Mary and Dickon had planted in spring are maturing into plants. Now with Colin, the three children watch stems extend, adding leaf—leaf—leaf, until at last flower buds

133

appear. Satin-petaled poppies bloom. The florets along snapdragons' stalks each look like a small toothed beast. The flowers of mignonettes are inconspicuous, but these "little darlings"—as the name translates from the French—infuse the air with a heady sweetness.

Plants that the children had tucked into the crevices and cracks of the garden's walls start "to unfurl and show color." They reveal their own secrets. The colors are varied, Burnett tells us, "every shade of blue, every shade of purple, every tint and hue of crimson." Note that there is no magenta in the secret garden, but more on that later.

Mary, Colin, and Dickon discover—much to everyone's surprise—that Ben Weatherstaff has been surreptitiously tending the roses for years, and he is brought into their clandestine pact. Remember that Mary and Dickon had decided to keep the garden on the unkempt side. Its beds are not overly tidy, and the grass is long, more meadow than lawn. Spiky sheaves of irises and whorls of pointed lily leaves rise up out of the grass. The green alcoves burgeon with blue and white flowers: campanulas, columbines, and tall delphiniums fluttering like "a bed o' blue an' white butterflies," according to Dickon.

The blue and white planting scheme was no accident. Ben Weatherstaff, it turns out, had been Mrs. Craven's gardener. We learn from Ben that Lilias Craven had been specific in her love of blue flowers, flowers that reflected the sky. This preference, not surprisingly, Burnett shared. Vivian later wrote that his mother "always wanted blue and white in her garden, and much of her time was spent in hunting up blue flowers that would blossom through the year."

A bed of delphiniums at Great Maytham Hall looks like
a congregation of blue butterflies.

Old garden roses clamber over the pergola at Great Maytham Hall
just like the cascades of roses in the secret garden.

Perhaps Burnett—nearing sixty years old and twice divorced—could also project herself into the character of a beloved wife who had loved her garden and died in youth.

If color preference is a window into a gardener's personality, then Frances's choice suggests a desire for a serenity. Blue is a peaceful color, calm and tranquil. With white, it connotes clear skies and white clouds, blue water and white sand. It is the combination that Chinese potters chose for their Ming porcelains and Delft potters for their earthenware. In flower beds, blue is cool on the eyes. Perhaps it is an unspoken secret of *The Secret Garden*.

One flower was unavailable in blue to either Burnett or her fictional creations. Roses come in white and in shades of red, pink, yellow, and orange, but not blue. Regardless of color constraint, the rose remained her favorite flower. It is the signature plant of *The Secret Garden*. The first summer that Mary, Colin, and Dickon work in the garden, the narrator gives a time lapse description of its roses, including their perfume:

> Rising out of the grass, tangled round the sun-dial, wreathing the tree trunks and hanging from their branches, climbing up the walls and spreading over them with long garlands falling in cascades—they came alive day by day, hour by hour. Fair fresh leaves, and buds—and buds—tiny at first but swelling and working Magic until they burst and uncurled into cups of scent delicately spilling themselves over their brims and filling the garden air.

137

Frances Hodgson Burnett, writing near the sundial in Maytham Hall's
rose garden, later included a rose-covered sundial in *The Secret Garden*.

The sundial centers the secret garden, as it had Maytham Hall's rose garden. It anchors with a solid reminder of time. Seasons change, plants bloom, grief dulls, and children grow. As summer edges into the first intimations of autumn, the garden inspires Colin Craven to try some magic of his own.

At Ben Weatherstaff's suggestion Dickon sings the Doxology, a traditional hymn of praise, to express thanks for the garden and Colin's return to health, illustrated by M. L. Kirk.

Where you tend a rose, my lad, /
A thistle cannot grow.

—*The Secret Garden*

A S SUMMER GREEN changes into autumn gold, the children tend the garden. And the garden tends the children. Each day, Colin intones, "Magic is in me! Magic is making me well!" Magic with a capital M is a steady refrain in the story, but it is neither sleight-of-hand nor the occult. Rather than black magic, it is green.

It is green of growth: roots, shoots, trees, flowers. It has that mossy smell, rich and old. "Oh! the things which happened in that garden!" exclaimed the narrator of *The Secret Garden*. "If you have never had a garden you cannot understand, and if you have had a garden you will know that it would take a whole book to describe all that came to pass there." The whole book is exactly what she wrote.

Burnett's philosophy in the story, her gardens, and her life was a custom blend. She called it "the Great Good Thing," casting a wide

141

The wonder of blue forget-me-nots, captured by artist Helen Sharp in 1895.

Borraginacea

Myosòtis

spiritual net. Her concept combined religion, positive thinking, an unsinkable belief in goodness, and an intense connection to nature. When Dickon's mother comes to see the children in their garden—their secret is safe with her—Mrs. Sowerby tells Colin that the "Good Thing" he is experiencing is "[t]h' same thing as sets th' seeds swellin' an' th' sun shinin'." The garden can heal the spirit, if not the body.

In the last few pages of *The Secret Garden*, action shifts to Archibald Craven, traveling to distract his mind from his sorrows, much as Frances had done after Lionel's death. We find Craven in the Alps, staring at the "wonders of blue" in a mass of forget-me-nots by a stream. His reactions to the landscape mirror Burnett's own encounters with nature. To Vivian, she had written in June 1910 on the ecstasy of wildflowers in the Italian Alps between Toblach and Cortina. "In the wonderful thick grass are billions of forget-me-nots, of yellow & purple pansies, of great kingcups & golden ranunculi, . . . of pink primulas—and above and beyond all—the two kinds of gentian." She found in nature an abundance to match her own. She found it in the months when she was completing *The Secret Garden*.

In the story, Archibald Craven travels from the mountains to the burnished autumn shores of Lake Como. There he dreams one night of his wife calling him. Startled awake, he hears her voice echoing, "In the garden," and again, "In the garden!" He thinks of Colin, still ill and sequestered in his ornate Misselthwaite bedroom—or so he believes. An unexpected letter arrives at the villa from Mrs. Sowerby, reading like a summons. Back to Yorkshire he rushes, through the

George S. Elg...

Frances gazes down on the face of the sundial in Maytham's rose garden.

opposite This illustration of a sundial in a rose garden appeared in Samuel Reynolds Hole's *A Book About Roses*, one of Frances's favorite gardening books.

European landscape to the secret garden and the satisfying conclusion of the book.

When Colin, Mary, and Dickon lead him through the hidden door, he steps into the garden, not just their garden, but also the garden that had belonged to him and his beloved Lilias. We now see it through Archibald Craven's newly opened eyes:

> The place was a wilderness of autumn gold and purple
> and violet blue and flaming scarlet and on every side
> were sheaves of late lilies standing together—lilies which
> were white or white and ruby. He remembered well when

the first of them had been planted that just at this season of the year their late glories should reveal themselves. Late roses climbed and hung and clustered and the sunshine deepening the hue of the yellowing trees made one feel that one stood in an embowered temple of gold.

The garden was very much alive, and so were Colin Craven, Archibald Craven, and Mary Lennox. Time had stopped for them, and it felt as though they were "going to live forever and ever and ever!"

A garden in memory is a powerful thing. In the wake of Burnett's last bittersweet visit to Maytham Hall, *The Secret Garden* germinated. Remembering, she could still sense the garden—the melody of birdsong, the potent fragrance of roses, the rough bark of the old apple trees. She could still walk from the door in the wall to her special table to the sundial and the gate in the laurel as if she were there in person. All she had to do was write it down.

Her friend, writer Ella Hepworth Dixon, understood the story from the first. They had often sat writing in the garden alongside one another on fine days at Maytham. To Ella, Frances confided that *The Secret Garden* "was our Rose Garden as it would have been if it had been locked up for years and years and years—and some hungry children had found it." Propelled by nostalgia for her rose garden and her robin, she wove in characteristics of people she had known—gardeners, household staff, and villagers.

Rather than turning it into an autobiographical novel, Burnett created something entirely new with *The Secret Garden*. Ella called the book "a children's Jane Eyre." With the magic carpet of her imagination, Burnett had moved the garden from Kent to Yorkshire—closer to her Manchester birthplace than her Rolvenden estate. She populated the garden with new leading characters—with the exception of the robin—and transformed its story into a classic.

PART THREE

after THE SECRET GARDEN

Mary at the door as the robin looks on, illustrated by Nora S. Unwin.

FOUR

NEST
BUILDING

PLANDOME PARK, NEW YORK
1909–1920

Her garden was her nest.

—*The Secret Garden*

B Y THE TIME Frances gave up the lease to Maytham Hall, she was already distracted by a new residential project. She had placed Vivian in charge of building a house on Long Island, a house that—in one way or another—they would share. He worked as an editor in Manhattan and wanted a weekend place on the water where he could sail. She wanted more time with him. After years of residing in England, she would move back to America. To Edith she confided, "It will be nice to feel one really has a home."

Mother and son chose Long Island's fashionable North Shore, within easy reach of New York City. (Some sources indicate that Frances became a naturalized American citizen around this time, perhaps to enable the property purchase.) Vivian had caught the fever for house and horticulture from "Dearest," and he contracted with New York architect William Tachau on her behalf.

Still in England and with Maytham fresh in her mind, Frances couldn't help comparing the plans for the new house to the Hall:

> Millions of money spent on a place in America would never give me what I felt that I walked into when I went out upon the terrace at Maytham—in fact I felt myself driving into it the moment we turned the pony in at the gate. It is a world which belongs to itself—a world where turf is velvet & unrolls itself in acres (instead of feet) where walls are old & beautiful & trees are great & thick & stand in mighty groups.

With some reservations, she signed the checks, and Vivian moved ahead with the contractors.

Maytham
Plandome Park
Manhasset, Long Island

Yours Sincerely

Frances Hodgson Burnett

1909

Burnett's first Long Island stationery, printed during construction of the house.

Like many construction projects, this one did not go entirely as planned. She later compared building a house to planting a flower that turned into a "seething, boiling, blasting, madly erupting" volcano, devouring everything in its path. During its construction, Frances traveled—to Austria, then to Germany to see the Passion Play, and on to Italy. By the middle of 1910, the house was complete, or at least habitable. She took up residence, and it remained her principal address for the rest of her life.

Her new Long Island home had something of an identity crisis. At first, Frances planned to repurpose the name "Maytham Hall." She even had stationery printed up. After all, no one from England could object, and perhaps she thought the reminder would be a balm. Soon, however, she abandoned the idea. In April 1910, she wrote Vivian that she had changed her mind. "I have decided to call the house 'The Garden' instead of Maytham. It will chiefly be a garden & sounds rather quaint." That name didn't stick either.

A year later, the Richmond, Virginia, *Times-Dispatch* published pictures of the house captioned "Famous Novelist and Her New Home" and called it "Plain View." Frances also tried out the name "Fairseat," which seems a better description for a property with a lovely curving waterfront. Finally, she settled on "Plandome Park," borrowing the name of the neighborhood. She settled into the idea of the house too.

Frances may have jokingly referred to the house as their Great Neck castle, but by Long Island standards of the day Plandome Park was modest. Long Island's so-called Gold Coast—think *Great*

Frances settled into her new house and "little garden" in 1910.

Gatsby—attracted owners with names like Vanderbilt, Frick, du Pont, and Guggenheim. They built castle-sized estates nearby. In contrast, Frances described Plandome Park as "only a little garden of three acres... on a pretty bay on Long Island, which makes it look much larger than it is." A path led up to the gracious, hip-roofed house with sunrooms on either side and deep eaves. The house faced northwest, positioned for sunset views over the protected bay that stretched into Long Island Sound. As at Maytham Hall, Plandome's spacious main hall opened onto a terrace that flanked the house. While Plandome could never be Maytham Hall for Frances, she made it her nest.

The Secret Garden launched in serial form in the November 1910 issue of *American Magazine*. Readers learned about Mary Lennox's nest just as Frances was feathering her own at Plandome Park. Burnett had used nests as a repeated refrain in *The Secret Garden*.

155

A Big New Serial

By Frances Hodgson Burnett

Author of

Little Lord Fauntleroy

The
Secret Garden

Be sure to begin The Secret Garden in the November American Magazine. It is a romance of youth as unique and absorbing as Little Lord Fauntleroy. It is difficult to describe this wonderful story. It is a story of mystery. There are in it three wonderful children and a great woman. It shows the magic of nature working under strange and romantic circumstances. It narrates the reformation and upbuilding of a life. It is a buoyant, joyous, thrilling story of youth—youth idealized as we would like to have it.

The Secret Garden is one of those universal romances unplaced and unplaceable, a delight for all that read, of any age.

Begins in the November Number of the
American Magazine

An advertisement for the 1910 launch of *The Secret Garden*.

Dickon mentions them first. When he steps through the ivy-covered door and sees the overgrown garden, he exclaims in wonder, "Eh! the nests as'll be here come springtime." The sheltered spot was perfect. "It'd be th' safest nestin' place in England," he tells Mary. "No one never comin' near an' tangles o' trees an' roses to build in. I wonder all th' birds on th' moor don't build here." He refers to the place as Mary Lennox's nest on more than one occasion, even leaving her a little sketch of a nesting bird as a coded message.

At Plandome, Frances began to create a garden varied in texture and color. Like a nest, she carefully enclosed it, planting trees and high hedges around its perimeter. She bracketed the terrace with roses and boxwood. Great arcs of azaleas and rhododendrons under-planted with nasturtiums encircled the lawns.

Frances added specimen evergreens and mixed flower borders facing the bay. There were banks of peonies for spring and "magnif-icent emperors of Oriental poppies" blooming red in summer; late in the growing season, there were single hardy chrysanthemums ("our salvation in autumn"), dahlias, and hydrangeas. Trimmed ever-greens separated the garden into rooms as in the "Land of the Blue Flower" with its rose-arched entrances, thick with annual larkspur and delphinium.

Delphiniums were prominent in *The Secret Garden*. Colin, whose father had given him many books, shared a volume about plants with Mary. He pointed to a picture and said in his imperious manner, "Those long spires of blue ones—we'll have lots of those.... They're called Del-phin-iums." No shrinking violet, Mary quotes her own

You can see why Frances had a weakness for delphiniums.

expert witness. "Dickon says they're larkspurs made big and grand," she replies. "There are clumps there already."

Like her characters, Frances loved delphiniums. They were her favorite color. They were tall. They were elegant and conspicuous. She planted them with fervor at Plandome Park. Vivian remembered that "delphiniums in later life were her greatest favorite, and her most heart-rending tragedy." He wrote:

> For one year in the side garden she grew delphiniums of the most stately kind[,] gorgeous in their blues of every shade, and with them pink roses that foamed over the borders of their beds at the first rush of June as if there were a wellspring of color beneath. It was a striking sight, beyond anything she had attained in England, and enough to make any gardener recklessly proud.

Pride, however, goeth before a fall, as the proverb goes.

Fast on the heels of the year of the delphinium came the delphinium blight, attracted no doubt by the monoculture—that is, too many plants of the same variety crowded together. It was heartbreaking for Frances. As the plants matured the following summer, their foliage blackened. Buds withered, along with her hopes for a repeat performance. She and Vivian tried everything to control the problem. For several years following, she replaced hundreds of plants. All in vain. She had to satisfy herself with dotting her blue borders with occasional clumps of delphiniums. The blight seemed to pass them by when they were planted among the other flowers.

By the time this photograph was taken, Frances was hiding her delphiniums among other flowers in the mixed borders to foil the blight which plagued them.

opposite Henderson supplied the Burnetts with many plants and seeds for Plandome Park's garden.

Plandome called for more plants. "A comfortable, rambling house is surrounded by gardens," said one writer of the place, "for which Mrs. Burnett buys flowers as uncontrollably as a bibliophile buys books." She had selected a neutral color for the exterior of the house, nested in among her colorful beds.

Frances spent winters poring over catalogues—Dreer's, Henderson's, and Kelsey's for perennials, Pierson's for roses, Gillett's

THE GARDEN BEAUTIFUL

EVERYTHING FOR THE GARDEN
1912
PETER HENDERSON & CO.
35 & 37 CORTLANDT ST., NEW YORK

Photographs of Maytham Hall and its gardens decorate Burnett's office at Plandome Park; cut flowers from her summer garden—lilies, delphiniums, iris, and phlox—fill two vases.

for hardy ferns. Of her routine, one journalist observed, "When a new seedman's catalogue arrives, other household affairs quite cease—such sordid matters as sleeping, writing books, eating and talking shop." Everything was put aside while new plantings were imagined, and orders prepared.

Both she and Vivian also appreciated the catalogues for their detailed plant information. A reputable nurseryman's or seedman's catalogue in the teens and twenties was a compendium of detailed gardening instruction, as appropriate for the novice as it was informative to the expert. One trick that they picked up was staggered planting of gladiola corms. By planting at intervals of a week or so during the spring, they could have prolonged bloom for the whole summer rather than a brief crescendo of gladioli with a sudden conclusion.

Crates arrived filled with alstroemerias, campanulas, single chrysanthemums, black-eyed susans, Shasta daisies, more roses, and many, many bulbs. Never a plant snob, she filled out the beds with what she termed "old-fashioned" annuals. She tucked in generous numbers to extend the bloom with flats of Orange King marigolds, *Phlox drummondii*, snapdragons, and Rosy Morn petunias. Summers in the gardens at Plandome Park were raucous with color. And let's not forget the zinnias.

Frances had a complicated relationship with zinnias. She liked to say that she had been "educated up" to them. They do not appear in *The Secret Garden*, so her change of heart occurred later, at Plandome Park. Whereas at first she'd considered them stiff and crude, she came to admire them—especially the giant ones, introduced around 1920.

Zinnias came in so many colors. They were as faithful as the sun, blooming with enthusiasm from early summer, growing taller than she was. Her zinnias were not the least bit fussy so long as they had enough bright light. The more she cut them for her bright bouquets, the more they flowered. In vases around the house she mixed them

Frances tucked a
list (opposite) of
rose selections for
her Welcome Bed at
Plandome Park into a
labeled envelope.

left Giant zinnia hybrids
converted Frances into
an enthusiast.

with delicate branches of spirea foliage to mask their stiff stems.
They lasted and lasted. In the garden they bloomed until frost extinguished them. She was completely converted.

While color was her byword, one hue was rejected. Frances had
an unexplained aversion to magenta. Vivian remembered that she
would humorously rail at catalogue descriptions that tried to foist a
variety upon her by euphemistically describing it as "rosy purple."
None of that for Frances. Thus *Petunia* 'Rosy Morn' (a soft rose pink)

Dean Hole - Silvery carmine, shaded salmon, flower large, variety of great excellence; useful for any purpose.

Etoile de France - velvety crimson, center vivid cerise red; carried on long erect stem, beautiful foliage, useful for cutting.

-Grace Darling - Creamy white, tinted & shaded with peach. Large & very floriferous.

-Gruss an Teplitz - Brightest scarlet crimson, very free flowering -

-Killarney - Flesh shaded white, suffused with pink. blooms large, buds long & pointed; fine for massing & forcing,

-Lyon Rose - Flowers large & globular, petals elegantly formed, the color a coral red or salmon pink shaded with chrome yellow in the center, very fragrant & hardy. A truly magnificent rose, absolutely distinct.

-Madame Jules Grolez - Bright china rose, flowers large & beautifully formed, very floriferous.

-Franceska Kruger - Coppery yellow, shaded with peach, large & full, useful for cutting.

-Madame Lombard - Bright rose, fine form, free bloomer.

-Marie van Houtte - Canary yellow, deeper center, border of petals tipped with rose.

The area around the garage was a blank canvas that Frances filled with more garden beds. (In the foreground is her Rolls-Royce town car.)

right The Plandome greenhouse, a delight for son and mother.

was welcome, while *P*. 'Howard's Star' (rosy crimson) was banned. Gardening, as with so many things in life, is subject to very personal preferences.

Even with all the other flowers, Frances always returned to roses. Like Lilias Craven and Mary Lennox in *The Secret Garden*, roses called to her with their beauty and fragrance. She and Vivian added more each year. "Please replace some of my roses with good roses if you can—Don't try experiments with new names at five dollars each. They are rarely ever new roses. I do want some more Red Radiance if I can get them. I need more red roses." She could never have enough.

The planting at the front of the house, her "Welcome Bed," skirted the main drive. At Maytham, it would have been the carriage entrance. By the time she built Plandome Park, times had changed. Car replaced carriage, chauffeur replaced coachman. Plandome had an elegant hip-roofed garage, detached from the house as was the custom. Each of the two garage bays featured double French doors with elliptical arched windows above the transoms.

On the south side of the garage, Frances added a sloping greenhouse. A 1912 article in *Country Life in America* featured this addition, describing it as an attractive structure of stucco and glass and noting that its lean-to style, albeit the cheapest form for a greenhouse, "harmonizes well with the garage and is in no sense an excrescence." A tad smaller than ten-by-twenty feet, it was perfect for propagation. Hundreds of packets of seeds arrived at Plandome each winter to be planted on the greenhouse benches, as the slatted tables are called, and grown on for the summer gardens.

167

Vivian loved the little greenhouse, and his mother gleefully encouraged his horticultural endeavors. "Is the greenhouse delighting your soul?" she inquired in one letter. On his weekends at Plandome, Vivian was her principal assistant, sourcing plants and supervising the help. He was serious about gardening: *The Craftsman* published his article "Craftsman Gardens for Craftsman Homes" in the April 1910 issue and "A Garden for the First Year" the following month.

Despite her son's growing skills, Frances seems to have had the final say on Plandome's gardens. One housekeeping note to him began thus: "*IMPORTANT. Are* the two Italians doing their work well?" She clarified, "If they are by this time everything should be perfectly weeded & the borders should be cut clean & spick & span. Please keep them up to it—please tell them that I am asking questions." The gardens were hers, though Vivian was her proxy.

As she had in the Maytham Hall gardens, Frances would put her guests to work. George Ettinger, dean of Muhlenberg College, spoke with personal insight of Plandome Park, observing that "respectable persons whose accustomed habit is a metropolitan club may be seen cheerfully removing wilted flower petals" from her gardens. Without a doubt, Frances made the job into something fun.

She still did plenty of the work herself, particularly deadheading, which she considered "master's work." This task wasn't merely to be tidy. Deadheading prolongs the blooms on most flowering plants; preventing the formation of seed signals the plants to keep blooming in order to reproduce. Deadheading tricks nature to benefit the gardener. Frances very much approved.

The cover of the first American edition of *The Secret Garden*, illustrated by M. L. Kirk.

Meanwhile, *The Secret Garden* was making its mark. In 1911, close on the heels of the magazine serialization, it came out in book form. At home and abroad, the notices were good. Not perhaps like *Fauntleroy*, but quite acceptable. One reviewer proclaimed the book "so quietly entertaining that you'll hate to hear your mother call you to supper."

More exciting to Frances were the letters she received from readers. They touched her heart. One in particular, from the father of a sick little girl named Frances, prompted an illuminating response:

Dear Little Namesake:

Someone who loves you very much has told me that you have been ill, and that you love "The Secret Garden," which I wrote. You see, I am Frances Hodgson Burnett, and "The Secret Garden" is my pet book. I never loved any book quite as much. I could scarcely bear to finish it.

I once had a home in England which was rather like Misselthwaite Manor. It was not in Yorkshire, nor among the moors, but it had been a Manor at the time of the Conquest, and it had a park around it and big trees, and old walled gardens, and one of the gardens was a rose garden, almost exactly like the Secret Garden—only it was not a secret. Roses grew over the trees and walls and there was a laurel-edged walk on one side of it, and a lovely wood with a little gate into it just like the one Mary went through when she found Dickon playing on his pipe.

Burnett fondly reminisced about the laurel-edged woodland alongside her rose garden at Maytham Hall.

right Roses continue to climb Maytham's garden walls, just as Burnett remembered.

An attentive robin painted by George Rankin
for *Britain's Birds and Their Nests* (1910).

I loved that garden more than any other place in the world. I used to sit under a twisted old apple tree covered with climbing roses and there I used to write books. All the birds knew me quite intimately, and didn't mind [my] being there at all—in fact, I think they liked me because I never moved quickly or made any noise. I used to come through a little green door in the wall just as Mary went into her garden and each of the five gardens opened into each other in the same way. It was while I was sitting writing under my tree one morning that my robin came to me, and I put this afterwards into the story of the Secret Garden. And it was because I loved my own garden so much that I wrote the story of Mary's. Afterwards I was asked to tell the real story of my real robin and so I wrote a little book about him, and I am sending it to you, and it is every word quite true.

Burnett's nonfiction account of her special English robin at Maytham Hall was published in 1912. She told her publisher that she was writing these "extras"—projects other than her novels—to fund her horticultural dreams. The income would "bloom next summer into a garden of blue delphiniums and roses such as was never before beheld." She could picture what Plandome might become.

That winter, Frances traveled once again to warmer climes, impatient for gardening weather. She had begun an annual winter migration, trading Long Island's icy gray days for a new place that would offer sunshine and more gardening possibilities.

Mary Lennox stepping into the secret garden, illustrated by Michael Halbert.

FIVE

A NEW BIT OF EARTH

CLIFTON HEIGHTS, BERMUDA
1912–1920

Roses & lilies & scarlet hibiscus are in bloom
now & all year—but—strangest of things!
The people seem to do nothing with their
gardens. You will see three rose bushes in
bloom where there might be three thousand.

—From a letter to Vivian during her first stay in
Bermuda, March 1911

A YEAR AFTER MOVING into her new home on Long Island, Frances decamped to Bermuda, that hook-shaped archipelago of sand and coral in the Atlantic, east of the Carolinas. It was a seasonal flight. She escaped the cold, exchanging gray skies of New York for Bermuda's brilliant blue. That year, in 1911, she stayed at the Princess Hotel, on the harbor waterfront in the city of Hamilton. She liked what she saw, but in her usual way longed for a home and garden to call her own. The following winter she rented a white bungalow called Clifton Heights, built of Bermuda coral. It was and still is located on Bailey's Bay, midway between Hamilton and St. George.

For ten succeeding years starting in 1912, Frances split her attention between two gardens, Plandome Park and Clifton Heights. One reporter described her typical year in these terms:

> When she leaves Plandome Mrs. Burnett consents to spend a few days in noisome New York—you can buy things there, after all, and editors and publishers there do congregate—and then she flees to Bermuda. But not until the last cosmos of autumn has perished and gone and every flowerbed at Plandome has been 'tucked in a blanket of fertilizer.' In Bermuda she—gardens.... Her Bermuda cottage is unpretentious but charming.

At this charming cottage with the help of a series of gardeners, she made a hillside garden.

The island soil is naturally thin—Frances termed it "wretched." To make beds in the upper garden, she enriched them with loads

Rather than donning her furs, Frances fled the cold to Bermuda's milder climes.

of manure, just as she had done in Kent. Of course, at Maytham Hall she and her friend Rosamund Campbell had done some of the digging themselves. Now in her sixties and beyond, she acted in a supervisory capacity. "I have had to stand by every shovelful & every moment," she told Vivian. The soil must be fully fed, she explained. "I wanted to leave good decent earth full of things which would make seedlings while I was away." The seedlings would have appreciated the attention, just as Dickon promised in *The Secret Garden*.

Clifton Heights, the white bungalow where Frances lived and gardened in Bermuda.

As at Plandome, Frances promoted color in her Bermuda garden. Her beds were full of yellow coreopsis, white candytuft, purple heliotrope, pink and white petunias, steely blue ageratums, and red poppies. Tall orange snapdragons grew in abundance. There were clouds of blue larkspur. In the mild climate, many annuals in her garden dropped seed and returned with vigor each year.

Acalypha wilkesiana dazzled Frances with its leaf color in her Bermuda borders.

far right Crotons made a vivid display for Frances at Clifton Heights.

Later in the season, sunflowers turned their red and gold heads to follow the track of each bright day. Cannas vied for height with the sunflowers, with statuesque leathery leaves and scarlet flowers. Pungent marigolds were one of her standbys; French varieties fringed the garden beds with lacy leaves and golden, crenelated petals.

Bermuda's subtropical weather gave her opportunities to try new plants. Bermuda suffers no frosts or freezes, thus fostering a broader plant palette. She learned to love crotons and bright-foliaged species of *Acalypha* (copperleaf). "The Acalifa [sic] and Aurantiums are as brilliant as the Crotons," she wrote to Vivian during her first winter at Clifton Heights, "and one could have quite a dazzling colorful garden

Hibiscus are superb plants for a subtropical garden, as Frances soon learned.

right Huge leaves of elephant ears (*Colocasia*) dominated shady spots in Burnett's back garden.

if one had not a flower in it." Elephant ears, aptly named, added statuesque weight to the shade of her back garden.

Despite her new enthusiasm for foliage, Frances added more and more flowers to her Bermuda borders. Red amaryllis bloomed in profusion and were hardy here. She cultivated many varieties of hibiscus, and bubbled in excitement to Vivian:

> Have you ever seen a Hibiscus in any greenhouse? They
> are superb things. They grow here into huge shrubs &
> bear great scarlet or pink blossoms or yellow ones. There
> are single & double ones—about four or five inches
> across. I planted four this morning about six or eight feet
> high & broad & full in proportion.

Hibiscus is the one flower Burnett mentioned by name in the first chapter of *The Secret Garden*, when Mary pretended to make a flower bed outside the Lennox family's Indian bungalow. Now she could grow them in her own garden. It seemed like a fairy dream.

Plant lust can get out of hand. Frances acquired many plants—shrubs, palms, and more—from the nursery at Bermuda's Agricultural Gardens. She encountered the results of her buying habits in a real way one day, returning to Bailey's Bay at the end of a carriage ride. The road was obstructed by what looked like a forest on wheels. She "imperiously" sent her driver to inquire after the cause of the delay. He returned to inform her that the convoy was her plant order, making its way by heavy cartloads from the nursery to Clifton Heights.

Frances also imported some familiar plant friends. Weigela bushes arrived from the mainland, beloved for their arched branches of pink and rose flowers. Forever enamored of roses, she got to know Agrippina and other cultivars suited to Bermuda. She laid out new rose beds in an area that she called the Secret Garden.

Clifton Heights was a heavenly place for a gardener to spend the winter. Frances had often tried to manage something like a Persephone act, retreating not to the underworld but to a sunny locale. While in England, it had been somewhere along the Mediterranean. Bermuda now served nicely, especially for a gardener. Seeds planted in November bloomed in February. By late March each year, Frances found herself enjoying the first days of a Bermuda summer. It was delightful, if a bit odd, to think about Vivian still in the clutches of a New York winter.

Here, too, she made special friends with the birds. At Clifton Heights were bluebirds, vireos—which she called "chick o' the village"—and her favorite, the redbirds or cardinals. She conversed with them on her daily rounds, throwing corn out on the grass for them each morning. Clifton Heights became for her "the place where the Redbirds sing." While no avian friend could ever compare to her particular English robin, she found the redbirds "almost as intimate."

After a few years of her ministrations and money, Clifton Heights started to look like a real garden. The head of Bermuda's public gardens admired her efforts, and Frances and her gardener began to enter local flower shows. When her sister Edith—now twice widowed—reached Bailey's Bay one season to open the house before her sister's arrival, she reported that she'd heard some of neighbors

The brilliant plumage of the redbird was very like the oleander that bloomed all over Bermuda and at the entrance to Clifton Heights.

say, "No one on the Island has flowers like Mrs. Burnett." What perfect news.

Clifton Heights was not entirely a vacation for Frances. Far from retired, she continued to work, publishing several novels and children's stories during these years. She had referred to herself as a "pen-driving machine" as far back as her Knoxville days, and nothing

Steaming into Bermuda on a winter day was pure joy for Frances.

much had changed except the tropical surroundings and her material possessions. She made a practice of writing in the morning, sitting indoors at her desk with pen in hand while the garden tempted her. Such dedication is the trial of every writer who gardens. A journalist shared that "she expects herself to work at her desk each morning though she confesses with a laugh that the lure of her gardens is at times irresistible."

Bermuda was divine. On arriving each year, she was met in a carriage—a double, pulled by two horses—and driven through a landscape of startling colors. White and turquoise. "As we drove along the shore I leaned back in the Victoria & said 'I believe I have died & wakened in Heaven.'" She loved its blue days. She loved the relaxed society—her Sunday afternoons became a must for the literary and horticultural sets. And she loved its island Englishness.

Settled into two houses and two gardens, one might suppose that Frances would have stowed her traveling shoes. Not so. She remained something of a wanderer. In a December 1912 letter, she outlined her plan to London friends, Ella and Madge Hepworth Dixon:

> I shall stay in Bermuda until my Spring Garden at
> Plandome Park is at full beauty—then I shall go and play
> in it—then I shall sail for England. I don't know what I
> shall do after that. Perhaps just wander. After a Bermuda
> winter, I may want some Alps.

She was restless for distraction, for refreshment, for material, or just for a change of scene.

Frances continued to crisscross the Atlantic, bound for distant shores. On one of her crossings, she met Elizabeth Jordan, a New York City–based author, editor, and suffragist fifteen years her junior. They'd been introduced before, but this time they clicked as if they'd been long-separated sisters. After evening meals, they shared conversation and confidences during strolls or in their cabins. One can imagine days of working or reading side by side on deck chairs. By 1915, their letters to one another open with "Querida" (Spanish for "dearest"), and this intimate friendship lasted for the rest of their lives.

Elizabeth Jordan
was editor of
Harper's Bazaar
when Frances
met her.

When the Great War made transatlantic crossings unsafe,
Burnett formed the habit of touring the eastern United States
and Canada, exploring new areas and staying at houses along the
Hudson River and in Quebec. She was especially taken by western
Massachusetts. She gave it her highest compliments. "One can find
England & the foothills of the Alps a few hours from New York—
and can motor into a country which gives one the feeling of being at

home," she wrote. "When one cannot cross the Atlantic one can go into the Berkshires." She had not known that there was such a place in America.

While on the surface the war seemed merely to alter her travel plans, it affected her deeply. She was heartsick for the world and consumed with worry for English friends and family. Her poem "From Leaf to Leaf" underscores her feelings, especially for those who grieved lost loved ones:

> *I held my grief when the leaves fell*
> *Close, close to my beating breast;*
> *"Sharp pain," I said, "great sorrow,*
> *To me God gives no rest!"*
> *The fierce thorns pierced my bosom,*
> *And burning drops of red*
> *Sprang with each anguished heart-throb,*
> *"But bring no peace," I said.*
>
> *My low and bitter sobbing*
> *Wearied both night and day;*
> *I cried in the heavy darkness,*
> *"Must it be thus alway?"*
> *Comes there no light with daybreak*
> *No rest when the sun is set?*
> *Must I for aye remember?*
> *God! can I ne'er forget?*

I held my grief when the leaves bud
Close—close to my silent heart;
"Sharp pain," I cried, "great sorrow,
Where is thine olden smart?"
I crushed the thorns 'gainst my bosom,
But there flowed no crimson tide,
Soft and slow were my heart-beats;
"Something is lost," I cried.

Then wild and fierce my sobbing
Broke on the fair spring day.
And I wailed with bitter passion,
"Must it be thus alway?"
What agony is like to this,
Oh, tears that fall so hot!
Not that I so remembered,
But that I so forgot!

Burnett's empathy with grief—borne of Lionel's loss—resurfaced with so many young men dying in Europe.

She cheered America's entry into the war, though she could never bring herself to encourage Vivian to enlist. After the war ended in 1918, she wrote to Rosamund Campbell, her friend from Maytham days, "The birds will sing and the buttercups will spread a gold carpet, and the hawthorn will bloom—and England will be England

The hawthorn tree, native to England, is a member of the rose family and blooms in May.

forever and ever and friends with all the world." (Frances would not live to see World War II.)

In those years, *The Secret Garden* blossomed in a brand-new medium. "I foresee that one is going to make a comfortable income by Film rights," she surmised, always attuned to mercenary prospects. By 1919, theatres around the country were showing a new Paramount picture, a silent film version of *The Secret Garden*. While Burnett was happy for the money, she left no indication of what she thought of the film or whether she had even seen it. In this case, she did not write the screenplay or dramatize the book for the stage as she had for most of her novels. This does not mean that she had forgotten the story.

MRS FRANCES
HODGSON BURNETT

Sunday
World

OF "LITTLE LORD FAUNTLE OY" "TH N OF

Burnett's earnings
and fame continued
into the age of
moving pictures.

opposite Frances
reading in the
sunroom at
Plandome Park
surrounded by
palms, ferns,
geraniums, and
a Norfolk Island
pine with an
arrangement of
roses on the desk.

From clues in her letters, it is clear that she kept *The Secret Garden* in mind. She wrote from Clifton Heights, "It seems strange in the midst of this summer flower garden to think of the bare beds & tiny green points just pushing through the earth at Plandome Park."

Frances kept both garden and weather in mind when planning her yearly calendar. She made every attempt to time her travels to avoid encounters with winter precipitation. Vivian was forewarned.

She would be savage, "very savage," if she returned to Plandome Park
only to encounter a blizzard—shades of Mary Lennox on a rainy day
at Misselthwaite. "I am afraid it would 'put one off' as they say in
England." Frances, I fear, was a fair-weather gardener. She usually
missed the early bulbs in her Long Island garden—snowdrops and
often daffodils—for fear of the cold.

In summer's warmth, she found Plandome Park adorable.
Frances cheerfully invited friends to visit and enjoy her gardens
there. Occasionally she held open days for the benefit of local chari-
ties. (While not active in any particular organization, she donated to

many causes, including the Woman Suffrage Party.) But oh, to her, her gardens could always look better. Just before company arrived, a storm would invariably batter the bloom or a hedge would suddenly look out of scale. Thank goodness, "the visitors who don't know its faults think it is wonderful."

As at Maytham Hall, she continually made improvements to her Long Island garden. A pergola provided a place to train wisteria. New arches were added. After Maytham, Frances never had another door in a wall to step through, but pergolas and arches served her needs.

She placed a fountain as a focal point, just as a fountain had been the centerpiece of the formal gardens that Mary explored at Misselthwaite Manor. A sea wall with a staircase and balustrade framed the edge of the beach. Two terraced lawns provided even more theatrical settings for her flowers.

For one major change at Plandome Park, Frances could take no credit. Vivian married a woman named Constance Buel in 1914. Frances saw nothing but delight ahead for the couple. She wrote to Constance's father, a retired editor at *Century Magazine*, that "they will go through life singing and playing together and growing roses in the summer." Above all, she insisted they be happy, and she would do everything in her power to ensure that outcome.

Vivian built a modest but comfortable home next door that he and Constance called "Bentleigh." Vivian continued to garden with his mother on the combined property, though he had to sequester his fruits and vegetables to a well-screened plot nicknamed the "Sneak Garden." Frances fiercely guarded the territory allotted to her flower

A fountain was one of the many features Frances added to her Plandome Park gardens.

opposite As at Plandome Park, the shade of a vine-covered archway contrasts with the bright border in this illustration from *The Joy of Gardens* (1911), which included a photograph of Burnett's garden in Kent.

beds. Whether through personal preference or wisdom in regard to mothers-in-law, it appears that Constance abstained from gardening all together. Besides, she had her hands full.

In short order, Mr. and Mrs. Vivian Burnett had two daughters: Verity in 1916 and Dorinda two years later. Grandchildren! Frances was elated with the joy that only they can confer. She lavished them

Red Oriental poppies inspired characters in games Frances played with her granddaughters.

below Frances gathering flowers from her autumn garden at Plandome with her granddaughter Verity.

with gifts and attention, and the girls loved her. One can imagine Frances and her storyteller's art focused on her two granddaughters. As Frances told Elizabeth Jordan, "I am Nanda, you know, and I am considered desperately fascinating. You see, *le bon Dieu* so made me that I can 'be' any number of persons at a moment's notice."

"Nanda" transformed her den into a playroom full of books and games, a tea set, and an elaborate dollhouse. Two families occupied the dollhouse, the Poppies and the Larkspurs:

> There is Mr. Poppy in scarlet velvet knickerbockers & silk hat and coat. Miss Poppy & a little sister Poppy & little broken Poppy. Mrs. Larkspur & an equal number of Larkspurs. Perhaps Mr. Poppy gave birth to all the Poppies and Mrs. Larkspur to all the Larkspurs—otherwise how account for the distinct coloring? They make quite showy parties sitting on the wicker chairs round the tea table.

Indoors and out, Frances shared the joys of flowers and gardening with a new generation.

Mary opening the ivy-covered door to the secret garden, illustrated by Scott McKowen.

WHEN THE SUN WENT DOWN

CLIFTON HEIGHTS & PLANDOME PARK
1921–1924

As long as one has a garden one has a future;
and as long as one has a future one is alive.

—From *In the Garden* (1924)

F RANCES HAD BEEN plagued with intermittent health problems since her first years of marriage. In 1921, during the season in Bermuda, her health took a downturn that seemed life-threatening. Edith was with her, but everyone was worried. Her condition concerned Vivian enough that he hastily arranged a trip from New York. Frances scribbled a reassuring letter as he prepared to come. She wrote sitting in a chair set in a shaded corner of the garden. Her gardener Billy was working nearby:

> I call feebly to Billy & he is making beds & planting things inspired by my impelling soul. I tell him you are coming & you know everything about gardens & will help him. Please bring Gillett's fern catalogue. There are places here too shady for anything but ferns.... Here is a strange thing. When I seemed to be actually dying there suddenly passed through my brain a new book & comedy in one. It was one of those gems which float about until they are ready to be written:

> No. 1. The Industrious Apprentice

> No. 2. A Transfusion of Blood.

Same old Frances, undaunted, full of garden plans and story ideas. Though that last one seems never to have gotten on paper. Too bad.

During Vivian's visit she slowly recovered strength, sharing her flowers and her redbirds with him. After he left, she sent him a

Frances gardened for shade as well as sun, with foliage as well as flower, as evidenced by her interest in the annual catalogue from Gillett's Hardy Fern and Flower Farm.

picture of herself in her sunny garden. He exhorted her to send him minute details of the garden's progress, as well as instructions for the plantings at Plandome.

By March she managed to get the seed order into Beddington's for spring annuals and to specify her ideas to Vivian, "The explanation of the large supply of mignonette is that I want to have the scent of it all over the garden.... Just scatter it & leave it to grow." Both Frances and Vivian were keen "noses," as scent specialists in the perfume industry are known. They understood how much the power of fragrance affected one's experience of a garden. Smell can transport us to other realms, to other times.

When she left Clifton Heights in 1921 to return to her late spring garden in New York, it would be the last time she saw Bermuda recede

Frances, pensive, leans on a wicker chair holding one of Plandome's peony blooms.

opposite Frances posing in the shade of her rose arch with a basket of delphinium.

in the wake of the steamer. Her remaining years would be spent closer to home, sometimes in New York City but mostly at Plandome.

Plandome continued to flower. Flowers adorned the house, growing outside and as bouquets inside. Frances continued to be generous with cut flowers for her friends, as she had been at Maytham Hall. In one of the hallway nooks at Plandome was a stack of green boxes, pre-stamped, to send garden flowers out by post. (Remember that mail was picked up and delivered twice a day in those years.)

Elizabeth Jordan was a frequent recipient of her floral largesse. One autumn, Frances sent her the very last "cold brave flowers" that she had picked. "The wonderful varied brilliant ones have died," she wrote in an enclosed note. "No, flowers don't die. They simply go to

Flower Heaven where I pray I may join them someday." She sensed that her own growing season was coming to an end as well and faced it calmly.

Frances owned a cemetery plot in nearby Roslyn, large enough for the family. They had buried Edith's husband Frank there after his tragic car accident in 1911, then Edith's son Ernest, a victim of the 1918 influenza pandemic. With Vivian, she sometimes referred to the plot as her "little house." She reminded him of one of her best-loved childhood Bible verses: "The repairer of the breach shalt

HENDERSON'S "ARTISTIC" COLLECTION OF CACTUS DAHLIAS

Cactus dahlias, which Frances had preferred since Maytham,
bloomed abundantly in her last October garden.

opposite A flourishing fall garden at Plandome boasted panicled
hydrangea standards, drifts of hardy chrysanthemums,
and the textures of conifers and ornamental grasses.

A statue of Lionel Burnett overlooks the family plot in Roslyn Cemetery.

thou be called, the builder up of waste places," and went on to say she would rather be that—a builder up of waste places—than anything else in the world. "Wouldn't you?" she asked, adding, "Let us put that over the portal of my 'little house' at Roslyn." It would indeed be the last of her many houses.

Doctors ultimately diagnosed Frances's digestive troubles as colon cancer. When able, she was still out in her gardens. Interviewing for a new head gardener, she complained that one of the candidates couldn't distinguish cabbages from wildflowers. But she finally found the right one. Extolling the virtues of her new hire, Samuel Thompson, she chortled to her beloved Elizabeth. "He is a Gardener. I have never had one in America. I have had Plumbers & Bricklayers & Chinese laundry men disguised as gardeners—But never a gardener," she wrote. "He is as passionate as I am. He wants as many flowers as I... Thompson & the garden have kept one from dying so far."

Two weeks before her death, she was entertaining guests in the garden. She would walk on Thompson's arm, pointing out tasks to be done and flowers to be cut for the house. In her final days, bed-ridden but pen still in hand, she finished the first of a planned series of articles on "Gardening for Everybody," intended for *The Country Gentleman*. She died in her bed at Plandome Park on 29 October 1924, aged seventy-four. Her grave at Roslyn stands in a copse of trees; a statue of Lionel seems to watch over it.

Late in her life, on stationery from Clifton Heights, Frances had copied out a familiar poem:

THE Lord God planted a garden
 In the first white days of the world,
And He set there an angel warden
 In a garment of light enfurled.

So near to the peace of Heaven,
 That the hawk might nest with the wren,
For there in the cool of the even
 God walked with the first of men.

And I dream that these garden-closes
 With their shade and their sun-flecked sod
And their lilies and bowers of roses,
 Were laid by the hand of God.

The kiss of the sun for pardon,
 The song of the birds for mirth—
One is nearer God's heart in a garden
 Than anywhere else on earth.

For He broke it for us in a garden
 Under the olive-trees
Where the angel of strength was the warden
 And the soul of the world found ease.

A discreet sign next to an elaborate wrought iron gate ushers visitors into the Secret Garden at Great Maytham Hall on garden open days.

Plandome Park's lovely view of Manhasset Bay, seen from Bayview Road.

The poem, "God's Garden," is by Dorothy Frances Gurney, a British poet and hymn writer. It was first published in London in 1913. Its verses capture Burnett's feelings for life in the garden, including her gardens—a lost one in Kent, a fictional one in Yorkshire, and her last two gardens on Long Island and Bermuda.

Of Burnett's gardens, only Great Maytham Hall remains, with its walls and pergola, its reinstalled ha-ha and extensive kitchen garden—all reminders of her passion for flowers and the scale on which she gardened. The Long Island property was left to her nephew Arthur "Archie" Fahnestock. He maintained the gardens, though he renamed the estate "Archways." Sadly, while he and his wife were on a cruise in December 1935, the house burned. Only the garage escaped the fire, but it too is gone now, replaced by a grand house (under construction as of this writing) on Bayview Road. The property retains its fine view of Manhasset Bay, though whether the new owners are gardeners remains to be seen. Clifton Heights is still there on its hill above Bailey's Bay in Bermuda, but its gardens have made way for a swimming pool.

Burnett's fictional garden lives on in many forms, from paper to bronze and everything in between. *The Secret Garden* has been reissued in many editions and adapted several times for stage and screen. My favorite is still the 1949 MGM film with Margaret O'Brien playing Mary Lennox. The movie opens in the rich cinematography of 1940s black and white, a grayscale palette suited to the death of Mary's parents in India and her introduction to the bleak Yorkshire moors and Misselthwaite Manor. When Mary finds the key and steps into the secret garden, the film pops into a full-color sequence. It's magic. (If this reminds you of Judy Garland's Dorothy waking up over the rainbow, that is because MGM used the same process for *The Wizard of Oz* a decade earlier.) I met a woman who remembered seeing *The Secret Garden* as a tiny girl, seated in a vast dark movie palace. She cherished that Technicolor memory. Other tributes and spinoffs include a *Secret Garden* cookbook, a board game, sticker books, a television series, a Tony Award–winning musical, a Madame Alexander doll depicting Mary Lennox, and, notably, the Burnett Memorial Fountain in New York's Central Park.

After her death, Vivian and Elizabeth Jordan formed a group of friends and colleagues to raise money and support for a Frances Hodgson Burnett memorial. The result is a bronze fountain, sculpted by Bessie Potter Vonnoh. For the subject, the committee chose Mary and Dickon from *The Secret Garden*. Water flows into a shallow basin held by Mary, with Dickon playing his flute nearby. The committee engaged landscape architect Charles Downing Lay to design the garden space surrounding the fountain.

In a 1927 article promoting the project, *New York Times* journalist Diana Rice emphasized that the memorial garden would function as a bird and nature sanctuary, and "belong to the children." Rice underscored Burnett's gardening interests and garden writing, and noted "she wrote lyrically, not pedantically, of brilliant blooms." Perhaps that is why *The Secret Garden* lasts.

The project did not go smoothly. For a time, the sculpture went into storage. Finally, on 28 May 1937, Mayor Fiorello La Guardia dedicated the memorial, set in a spot near 105th Street and Fifth Avenue. It is now a part of the Conservatory Garden, restored by Lynden B. Miller and the Central Park Conservancy in 1983. The fountain is surrounded by an English garden. Spring and summer, birds drink and bathe in its steady trickle. Children run and laugh, as children should.

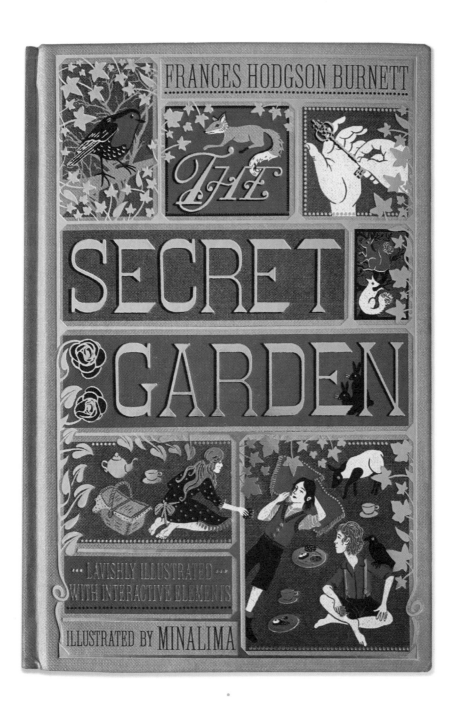

A recent edition of *The Secret Garden* with a fresh look and interactive elements.

The Secret Garden fountain in Central Park's Conservatory Garden
pays ongoing tribute to the book and its author.

Frances Hodgson Burnett gardened as she lived—large—and became the unlikely inspiration for generations of gardeners through *The Secret Garden*. She unlocked a door that beckons. If you ask a gardener if they have a book—in particular a childhood book—that led them into gardening, many of them would name *The Secret Garden*. Frances would be pleased.

PART FOUR

outside THE SECRET GARDEN

Burnett working at her writing desk in Plandome Park, c.1920.

SEVEN

FURTHER GARDEN WRITINGS

of

FRANCES HODGSON BURNETT

COUNTRY LIFE
IN AMERICA

VOLUME X—NUMBER 3   July, 1906   PRICE, 35 CENTS
$4 A YEAR POSTPAID

Here is the ha-ha, the clever device of some old gardener for keeping the park deer from the lawn without resorting to an ugly fence or hedge. Looking across it from the lawn at the left, it is hardly visible

The magazine banner and lead photograph for Burnett's article in *Country Life in America.*

BURNETT'S GARDENING WRITING was not limited to *The Secret Garden*, though the others are little known. To remedy that, here is a collection of the best of her nonfiction "extras" in chronological order. The first is an article from *Country Life in America* about a special feature of Maytham Hall's landscape. The next, originally a small book, concerns a special bird at Maytham Hall. The crescendo is an enthusiastic essay that shares the bubbling joy of gardening from someone who, by the time she wrote it, had gardened for more than a quarter of a century.

Burnett's Kentish landscape boasted that most English of garden elements, the ha-ha. *The Baltimore Sun* reported, "Mrs. Burnett has come into possession of a 'ha-ha' in her beautiful estate, Mayth[a]m Hall, in Kent, England." While it may be among the silliest of landscape terms, Burnett was delighted to have one, at least at first.

A ha-ha is a wide, deep depression sunk into the grade of a property. It acts as a boundary, but the view is unobstructed. No wall, no fence, no hedge, just a long, lovely view. Done properly, the artful result looks like a landscape painting. If livestock grazed in the park—cows, for example—the ha-ha had to be big enough to prevent their crossing. The lawn closest to the house remained unsullied by excrement, with the animals arranged at an artful distance. Burnett once mentioned sheep at Maytham Hall, so its ha-ha was practical as well as aesthetic.

Popularized in the eighteenth century, the ha-ha makes frequent appearances in English novels including Jane Austen's *Mansfield Park*, though not—one must report—in Burnett's. Maytham's ha-ha might have been installed when the house was built, though there's no record to prove it. Frances did document when she removed it. Though she was only a tenant, Frances made the garden her own.

221

Within a year of signing the lease, she had tired of the ha-ha, so out it went. She asked Edith:

> *Have* I told you about the alterations which have been made at the South front of the Hall? They are such an improvement. The Ha Ha has been removed and the whole expanse leveled & smoothed with a great velvet lawn, the hedge by the Rose Walk has been removed & the tangle of shrubs cleared a little so that now flower beds open on to the lawn on that side.

Despite eliminating the ha-ha, she penned an article about it for *Country Life in America*.

The article was called "An American Author's English Ha-ha." An English woman by birth, and an American by circumstance, Frances Hodgson Burnett is still claimed as an author by both countries. In the title to this piece she asserted "American," though perhaps that was to match the interests of the particular periodical.

Burnett was always alert to an opportunity for monetizing her experiences. Magazines like *Country Life* featured photography, which meant that both she and Vivian could be involved in the project. Frances encouraged his artistic endeavors—music, photography, writing, and later, gardening—as appropriate accomplishments for her gentleman son. Besides, while they were considering plans for their new property on Long Island, they could make some money on the one she was about to leave behind.

AN AMERICAN AUTHOR'S ENGLISH HA-HA

BY FRANCES HODGSON BURNETT

PHOTOGRAPHS BY VIVIAN BURNETT

·

What is a ha-ha?—How Mrs. Burnett finally discovered the meaning of an elusive term sometimes found in English novels— A device useful for other purposes than romance

"THE PARK IS divided from the gardens by a ha-ha." This statement made in the agent's catalogue was perhaps the chief reason for my deciding to obtain an "Order to View," and journey down into Kent, to see the estate described with much picturesqueness in the catalogue in question. Certain details, including "two hundred acres of undulating, beautifully timbered park, lovely

223

top "The Hall, large, gabled, agreeably rambling and about two centuries old," with its broad shady lawn and ancient cedar sentinels.

below The borders in summer are alive with color, and there are bees among the sweet peas, lilies and phloxes.

old walled gardens, ancient stone terrace, ornamental lake," were attractive, but concerning the ha-ha I burned with curiosity. I had never had a ha-ha. I had never even seen one. I had, however, read several English novels in which one was mentioned, though never explained. The only gleam of light I had ever obtained had come from a scene in such a novel, in which it was—most casually—stated that the hero "leapt lightly across the ha-ha," to join the heroine on the other side.

MAYTHAM HALL

Upon the whole, I went down into Kent, looking forward to making clear to myself at last how it was done, why, and at what personal risk.

I found the house or, rather, Hall, as it was called, large, gabled, agreeably rambling and about two hundred years old. A manor house had stood in its place, one is told, at the time of the Conquest. The kitchen gardens and a sort of turfed court, known as the kennel yard, where a pack of hounds had been originally kept in a row of what looked like small, whitewashed brick cottages, were enclosed by ancient red walls, with the curious gray bloom of old upon them, and with pear and peach and plum and nectarine trees spread and trained flat against them in good old English garden fashion. In the clefts of the wall lovely green and yellow bunches of things grew, and trailing creepers, entirely unprovoked; on the flagged tops, in some most mysterious way, here and there, small cedar bushes had taken root and apparently throve on nothing whatever but Kentish air and brick and mortar.

225

A KENTISH GARDEN

The ornamental lake was to be found in the "beautifully timbered and undulating park," according to catalogue; there was a long Rose Walk and tangled flower gardens. One stepped from the south hall door on to the broad, ancient stone terrace, and when one stood upon it there spread before one a view of half the Weald of Kent. From the terrace a short flight of lichen-covered stone steps led to the lawns and to the flower gardens, but even when I descended them I saw for some minutes nothing which could be construed into a ha-ha. Temporarily it appeared that the catalogue had deceived me and raised false hopes only to dash them to earth. But when I walked out upon the great turfed spaces and approached the point where they joined the park, I found that I had not been misled. The ha-ha was there, and when I saw it I realized (I must confess with some assistance from the head gardener) its utilitarian purpose and meaning.

WHAT A HA-HA IS

Literally it is an extremely clever arrangement of the landscape gardener of long ago (or one may suppose he was of long ago, as the ha-ha is found oftenest in old places), and it is the device of one who dealt with English gardens attached to broad English private parks. Its *raison d'être* is the following:

In most private parks, deer, cattle or sheep are usually pastured, partly for the utilitarian purpose of fertilization and close cropping of the turf, and partly because of their forming a picturesque detail. Deer are obviously ornamental, so are fine cattle, especially small herds of the shaggy black Highland bulls, or stag-eyed Jerseys, and nothing produces a more softly completing effect than a scattered flock of snow-white sheep, straying and nibbling or resting in groups under spreading boughs of oaks and beeches. From these, of course, the garden must be protected by some sufficient barrier, and for this purpose the ha-ha was invented.

A feature of most park-surrounded pleasure grounds is that it has been part of the designer's plan that they shall not appear to be limited by any stretch of fence or hedge which would break the line of sight, but that the garden shall produce the effect of melting into the sward of the park and seem to be part of its broad sweeps and spaces. A hedge or fence would form an obvious boundary, and the ha-ha was the ingenious alternative.

HOW IT IS MADE

A dry moat is dug where lawns join park lands. One side, that toward the lawns, is perpendicular; the other gently slopes; the tops are carefully levelled with each other, and the whole neatly turfed. The perpendicular side is usually fitted with a short horizontal fence of wire netting to prevent the incursions of rabbits. No animal can cross this, and when it is carefully levelled, the result achieved is that, even when one stands at a distance of only a few yards from it, the eye notes no break in the sweep of the turf and sees nothing of the barrier, either depression or fencing, the moat being below the line of view instead of forming a limiting obstruction to it.

THE FLOWERS AT MAYTHAM

In the turf of the one at Maytham I have planted many bulbs of white *narcisse de poete*, jonquils and daffodils, which lie asleep during the summer and winter and pierce through the grass each spring, requiring no more attention than buttercups and daisies. They were thrust into the earth without ceremony seven or eight years ago and have been undisturbed ever since. Neither rabbits nor sheep seem to nibble them.

Since I have possessed a ha-ha of my own I have met many people who are as interested and as vague as I myself once was, and when asked to explain the matter I have felt—judging from my own past emotions—that to do so would perhaps be to allay a desire for elucidation as keen as was my own.

THE ORIGIN OF THE WORD "HA-HA"

Concerning the original meaning of the name ha-ha I do not feel that I have yet been satisfactorily enlightened. Dean Reynolds Hole, in one of his famous garden books, gives this story as the solution of the mystery: "An individual being brought without warning to the edge of the first specimen of barrier, on suddenly finding it yawning at his feet, cried out in delighted amazement, 'Ha-Ha!'." But this to the perfervid romantic mind seems *banale*. For myself I should prefer an explanation more picturesque and early English. But so far one only knows that the thing is called a ha-ha.

Each spring, many varieties of daffodils still brighten Maytham's borders.

over "In the clefts of the wall lovely green and yellow bunches
of things grew, and trailing creepers, entirely unprovoked;
on the flagged tops, here and there small cedar bushes had taken root
and throve on Kentish air."

CONNECTING WITH NATURE:
MY ROBIN
(1912)

When *My Robin* came out in 1912, the publisher couldn't keep up with demand from the buying public. It is Burnett's recollection of a precocious bird, the real robin that inspired its fictional counterpart in *The Secret Garden*.

In September 1899 during her tenure at Maytham Hall, Frances wrote to her friend Annie Russell about writing in the garden "with roses and robins coming to inquire." She observed, "I find that robins are fond of human society—if it is nice human society such as I am composed of. They want to talk to you about their families & come hopping about your feet to begin intimacies." Frances made a particular connection with one of these sociable birds.

More than a decade later, Burnett captured her memories in book form as *My Robin*. In correspondence with her publisher, she was adamant that her robin was a real person. Her respect for her avian friend is clear throughout the short book.

Without the robin, Mary Lennox might not have found the key or unlocked the door to the secret garden. And perhaps without her robin, Burnett might not have found the key to her classic story.

The Robin sings in the rose garden as Frances and her gardener
look on, illustrated by Alfred Brennan.

MY ROBIN

BY FRANCES HODGSON BURNETT

ILLUSTRATIONS BY ALFRED BRENNAN

T HERE CAME TO me among the letters I received last spring one which touched me very closely. It was a letter full of delightful things but the delightful thing which so reached my soul was a question. The writer had been reading "The Secret Garden" and her question was this: "Did you own the original of the robin? He could not have been a mere creature of fantasy. I feel sure you owned him." I was thrilled to the centre of my being. Here was some one who plainly had been intimate with robins—English robins. I wrote and explained as far as one could in a letter what I am now going to relate in detail.

I did not own the robin—he owned me—or perhaps we owned each other.

He was an English robin and he was a *person*—not a mere bird. An English robin differs greatly from the American one. He is much smaller and quite differently shaped. His body is daintily round and plump, his legs are delicately slender. He is a graceful little patrician with an astonishing allurement of bearing. His eye is large and dark and dewy; he wears a tight little red satin waistcoat on his full round breast and every tilt of his head, every flirt of his wing is instinct with dramatic significance. He is fascinatingly conceited—he burns with curiosity—he is determined to engage in social relations at almost any cost and his raging jealousy of attention paid to less worthy objects than himself drives him at times to efforts to charm and distract which are irresistible. An intimacy with a robin—an English robin—is a liberal education.

This particular one I knew in my rose-garden in Kent. I feel sure he was born there and for a summer at least believed it to be the world. It was a lovesome, mystic place, shut in partly by old red brick walls against which fruit trees were trained and partly by a laurel hedge with a wood behind it. It was my habit to sit and write there under an aged writhen tree, gray with lichen and festooned with roses. The soft silence of it—the remote aloofness—were the most perfect ever dreamed of. But let me not be led astray by the garden. I must be firm and confine myself to the Robin. The garden shall be another story.

There were so many people in this garden—people with feathers, or fur—who, because I sat so quietly, did not mind me in the least, that it was not a surprising thing when I looked up one summer morning to see a small bird hopping about the grass a yard or so away from me. The surprise was not that he was there but that he *stayed* there—or rather he continued to hop—with short reflective-looking hops and that while hopping he looked at me— not in a furtive flighty way but rather as a person might tentatively regard a very new acquaintance. The absolute truth of the matter I had reason to believe later was that he did not know I was a person. I may have been the first of my species he had seen in this rose-garden world of his and he thought I was only another kind of robin. I was too—though that was a secret of mine and nobody but myself knew it. Because of this fact I had the power of holding myself *still*—quite *still* and filling myself with softly alluring tenderness of the tender- est when any little wild thing came near me.

"What do you do to make him come to you like that?" some one asked me a month or so later. "What do you *do*?"

"I don't know what I do exactly," I said. "Except that I hold myself very still and feel like a robin."

You can only do that with a tiny wild thing by being so tender of him—of his little timidities and feelings—so adoringly anxious not to startle him or suggest by any movement the possibility of your being a creature who *could hurt*—that your very yearning to under- stand his tiny hopes and fears and desires makes you for the time cease to be quite a mere human thing and gives you another and more exquisite sense which speaks for you without speech.

As I sat and watched him I held myself softly still and felt just that. I did not know he was a robin. The truth was that he was too young at that time to look like one, but I did not know that either. He was plainly not a thrush, or a linnet or a sparrow or a starling or a blackbird. He was a little indeterminate-colored bird and he had no red on his breast. And as I sat and gazed at him he gazed at me as one quite without prejudice unless it might be with the slightest tinge of favor—and hopped—and hopped—and hopped.

That was the thrill and wonder of it. No bird, however evident his acknowledgment of my harmlessness, had ever hopped and *remained*. Many had perched for a moment in the grass or on a nearby bough, had trilled or chirped or secured a scurrying gold and green beetle and flown away. But none had stayed to inquire—to reflect—even to seem—if one dared be so bold as to hope such a thing—to make mysterious, almost occult advances towards intimacy. Also I had never before heard of such a thing happening to any one howsoever bird loving. Birds are creatures who must be wooed and it must be delicate and careful wooing which allures them into friendship.

I held my soft stillness. Would he stay? Could it be that the last hop was nearer? Yes, it was. The moment a breathless one. Dare one believe that the next was nearer still—and the next—and the next—and that the two yards of distance had become scarcely one—and that within that radius he was soberly hopping round my very feet with his quite unafraid eye full upon me. This was what was happening. It may not seem exciting but it was. That a little wild thing should come to one unasked was of a thrillingness touched with awe.

237

Without stirring a muscle I began to make low, soft, little sounds to him—very low and very caressing indeed—softer than one makes to a baby. I wanted to weave a spell—to establish mental communication—to make Magic. And as I uttered the tiny sounds he hopped nearer and nearer.

"Oh! to think that you will come as near as that!" I whispered to him. "You *know*. You know that nothing in the world would make me put out my hand or startle you in the least tiniest way. You know it because you are a real person as well as a lovely—lovely little bird thing. You know it because you are a soul."

Because of this first morning I knew—years later—that this was what Mistress Mary thought when she bent down in the Long Walk and "tried to make robin sounds."

I said it all in a whisper and I think the words must have sounded like robin sounds because he listened with interest and at last—miracle of miracles as it seemed to me—he actually fluttered up on to a small shrub not two yards away from my knee and sat there as one who was pleased with the topic of conversation.

I did not move of course, I sat still and waited his pleasure. Not for mines of rubies would I have lifted a finger.

I think he stayed near me altogether about half an hour. Then he disappeared. Where or even exactly when I did not know. One moment he was hopping among some of the rose bushes and then he was gone.

This, in fact, was his little mysterious way from first to last. Through all the months of our delicious intimacy he never let me know where he lived. I knew it was in the rose-garden—but that was all. His extraordinary freedom from timorousness was something to think over. After reflecting upon him a good deal I thought I had reached an explanation. He had been born in the rose-garden and being of a home-loving nature he had declined to follow the rest of his family when they had made their first flight over the wall into the rose-walk or over the laurel hedge into the pheasant cover behind. He had stayed in the rose world and then had felt lonely. Without father or mother or sisters or brothers desolateness of spirit fell upon him. He saw a creature—I insist on believing that he thought it another order of robin—and approached to see what it would say.

Its whole bearing was confidence inspiring. It made softly alluring—if unexplainable—sounds. He felt its friendliness and affection. It was curious to look at and far too large for any ordinary nest. It plainly could not fly. But there was not a shadow of inimical sentiment in it. Instinct told him that. It admired him, it wanted him to remain near, there was a certain comfort in its caressing atmosphere. He liked it and felt less desolate. He would return to it again.

The next day summer rains kept me in the house. The next I went to the rose-garden in the morning and sat down under my tree to work. I had not been there half an hour when I felt I must lift my eyes and look. A little indeterminate-colored bird was hopping quietly about in the grass—quite aware of me as his dew-bright eye manifested. He had come again—of intention—because we were mates.

It was the beginning of an intimacy not to be described unless one filled a small volume. From that moment we never doubted each other for one second. He knew and I knew. Each morning when I came into the rose-garden he came to call on me and discover things he wanted to know concerning robins of my size and unusual physical conformation. He did not understand but he was attracted by me. Each day I held myself still and tried to make robin sounds expressive of adoring tenderness and he came each day a little nearer. At last arrived a day when as I softly left my seat and moved about the garden he actually quietly hopped after me.

I wish I could remember exactly what length of time elapsed before I knew he was really a robin. An ornithologist would doubtless know but I do not. But one morning I was bending over a bed of Laurette Messimy roses and I became aware that he had arrived in his usual mysterious way without warning. He was standing in the grass and when I turned my eyes upon him I only just saved myself from starting—which would have meant disaster. I saw upon his breast the first dawning of a flush of color—more tawny than actual red at that stage—but it hinted at revelations.

"Further subterfuge is useless," I said to him. "You are betrayed. You are a robin."

And he did not attempt to deny it either then or at any future time. In less than two weeks he revealed a tight, glossy little bright red satin waistcoat and with it a certain youthful maturity such as one beholds in the wearer of a first dress suit. His movements were more brisk and certain. He began to make little flights and little

"A heavenly rush of wings."

sounds though for some time he made no attempt to sing. Instead of appearing suddenly in the grass at my feet, a heavenly little rush of wings would bring him to a bough over my head or a twig quite near me where he would tilt daintily, taking his silent but quite responsive part in the conversations which always took place between us. It was I who talked—telling him how I loved him—how satin red his waistcoat was—how large and bright his eyes—how delicate and elegant his slender legs. I flattered him a great deal. He adored flattery and I am sure he loved me most when I told him that it was impossible to say anything which *could* flatter him. It gave him confidence in my good taste.

One morning—a heavenly sunny one—I was conversing with him by the Laurette Messimys again and he was evidently much pleased with the things I said. Perhaps he liked my hat which was a large white one with a wreath of roses round its crown. I saw him look at it and I gently hinted that I had worn it in the hope that he would approve. I had broken off a handful of coral pink Laurettes and was arranging them idly when—he spread his wings in a sudden upward flight—a tiny swift flight which ended—among the roses on my hat—the very hat on my head.

Did I make myself still then? Did I stir by a single hairbreadth? Who does not know? I scarcely let myself breathe. I could not believe that such a thing of pure joy could be true.

But in a minute I realized that he at least was not afraid to move. He was perfectly at home. He hopped about the brim and examined the roses with delicate pecks. That I was under the hat apparently only gave him confidence. He knew me as well as that. He stayed until he had learned all he wished to know about garden hats and then he lightly flew away.

From that time each day drew us closer to each other. He began to perch on twigs only a few inches from my face and listen while I whispered to him—yes, he *listened* and made answer with chirps. Nothing else would describe it. As I wrote he would alight on my manuscript paper and try to read. Sometimes I thought he was a little offended because he found my handwriting so bad that he could not understand it. He would take crumbs out of my hand, he would alight on my chair or my shoulder. The instant I opened the little door in the leaf-covered garden wall I would be greeted by the darling little rush of wings and he was beside me. And he always came from nowhere and disappeared into space.

That, through the whole summer—was his rarest fascination. Perhaps he was not a real robin. Perhaps he was a fairy. Who knows? Among the many house parties staying with me he was a subject of thrilled interest. People knew of him who had not seen him and it became a custom with callers to say: "May we go into the rose-garden and see The Robin?" One of my American guests said he was uncanny and called him "The Goblin Robin." No one had ever seen a thing so curiously human—so much more than mere bird.

When I took callers to the rose-garden he was exquisitely polite. He always came when I stood under my tree and called—but he never at such times *met* me with his rush to the little door. He would

243

He was perched on a rib of the Japanese umbrella.

perch near me and talk but there was a difference. Certain exquisite intimate charms he kept for me alone.

I wondered when he would begin to sing. One morning the sun being strong enough to pierce through the leaves of my tree I had a large Japanese tent umbrella arranged so that it shaded my table as I wrote. Suddenly I heard a robin song which sounded as if it were being trilled from some tree at a little distance from where I sat. It was so pretty that I leaned forward to see exactly where the singer perched. I made a delicious discovery. He was not on a tree at all. He was perched upon the very end of one of the bamboo ribs of my big flowery umbrella. He was my own Robin and there he sat singing to me his first tiny song—showing me that he had found out how to do it.

The effect of singing at a distance was produced by the curious fact that he was singing *with his bill closed*, his darling scarlet throat puffed out and tremulous with the captive trills.

Perhaps a robin's first song is always of this order. I do not know. I only know that this was his "earlier manner." My enraptured delight I expressed to him in my most eloquent phrases. I praised him—I flattered him. I made him believe that no robin had really ever sung before. He was much pleased and flew down on to the table to hear all about it and incite me to further effort.

In a few days he had learned to sing perfectly, not with the low distant-sounding note but with open beak and clear brilliant little roulades and trills. He grew prouder and prouder. When he saw I was busy he would tilt on a nearby bough and call me with flirtatious, provocative outbreaking of song. He knew that it was impossible for any one to resist him—any one in the world. Of course I would get up and stand beneath his tree with my face upturned and tell him that his charm, his beauty, his fascination and my love were beyond the power of words to express. He knew that would happen and revelled in it. His tiny airs and graces, his devices to attract and absorb attention was unending. He invented new ones every day and each was more enslaving than the last.

Could it be that he was guilty—when he met other robins— of boasting of his conquest of me and of my utter subjugation? I cannot believe it possible. Also I never saw other robins accost him or linger in their passage through the rose-garden to exchange civilities. And yet a very strange thing occurred on one occasion. I was sitting at my table expecting him and heard a familiar chirp. When I looked up he was atilt upon the branch of an apple tree near by. I greeted him with little whistles and twitters thinking of course that he would fly down to me for our usual conversation. But though he chirped a reply and put his head on one side engagingly he did not move from his bough.

"What is the matter with you?" I said. "Come down—come down, little brother!"

But he did not come. He only sidled and twittered and stayed where he was. This was so extraordinary that I got up and went to him. As I looked a curious doubt came upon me. He looked like Tweetie—(which had become his baptismal name) he tilted his head and flirted and twittered after the manner of Tweetie—but—could it be that he was *not* what he pretended to be? Could he be a stranger bird? That seemed out of the question as no stranger bird would have comported himself with such familiarity. No stranger surely would have come so near and addressed me with such intimate twitterings and well-known airs and graces. I was mystified beyond measure. I exerted all my powers to lure him from his branch but descend from it he would not. He listened and smiled and flirted his tail but he stayed where he was.

"Listen," I said at last. "I don't believe in you. There is a mystery here. You pretend you know me and yet you act as if you were afraid of me—just like a common bird who is made of nothing but feathers. I don't believe you are Tweetie at all. You are an Impostor!"

Believable or not, just at that moment when I stood there under the bough arguing, reproaching and beguiling by turns and puzzled beyond measure—out of the Nowhere darted a little scarlet flame of frenzy—Tweetie himself—with his feathers ruffled and on fire with fury. The robin on the branch actually *was* an Impostor and Tweetie had discovered him red-breasted if not red-handed with crime. Oh! the sight it was to behold him in his tiny Berseker rage at his impudent rival. He flew at him, he beat him, he smacked him, he pecked him, he shrieked bad language at him, he drove him from the branch—from the tree, from one tree after another as the little traitor tried to take refuge—he drove him from the rose-garden—over the laurel hedge and into the pheasant cover in the wood. Perhaps he killed him and left him slain in the bracken. I could not see. But having beaten him once and forever he came back to me, panting—all fluffed up—and with blood thirst only just dying in his eye. He came down on to my table—out of breath as he agitatedly rearranged his untidy feathers—and indignant—almost unreconcilable because I had been such an undiscriminating and feeble-minded imbecile as to be for one moment deceived.

His righteous wrath was awful to behold. I was so frightened that I felt quite pale. With those wiles of the serpent which every noble woman finds herself forced to employ at times I endeavored to pacify him.

"Of course I did not really believe he was You," I said tremulously. "He was your inferior in every respect. His waistcoat was not nearly so beautiful as yours. His eyes were not so soul compelling. His legs were not nearly so elegant and slender. And there was an expression about his beak which I distrusted from the first. You *heard* me tell him he was an Impostor."

He began to listen—he became calmer—he relented. He kindly ate a crumb out of my hand.

We began mutually to understand the infamy of the situation. The Impostor had been secretly watching us. He had envied us our happiness. Into his degenerate mind had stolen the darkling and criminal thought that he—Audacious Scoundrel—might impose upon me by pretending he was not merely "a robin" but "The Robin"—Tweetie himself and that he might supplant him in my affections. But he had been confounded and cast into outer darkness and again we were One.

I will not attempt to deceive. He was jealous beyond bounds. It was necessary for me to be most discreet in my demeanor towards the head gardener with whom I was obliged to consult frequently. When he came into the rose-garden for orders Tweetie at once appeared.

He followed us, hopping in the grass or from rose bush to rose bush. No word of ours escaped him. If our conversation on the enthralling subjects of fertilizers and aphides seemed in its earnest absorption to verge upon the emotional and tender he interfered at once. He commanded my attention. He perched on nearby boughs and endeavored to distract me. He fluttered about and called me with chirps. His last resource was always to fly to the topmost twig of an apple tree and begin to sing his most brilliant song in his most thrilling tone and with an affected manner. Naturally we were obliged to listen and talk about him. Even old Barton's weather-beaten apple face would wrinkle into smiles.

"He's doin' that to make us look at him," he would say. "That's what he's doin' it for. He can't abide not to be noticed."

But it was not only his vanity which drew him to me. He loved me. The low song trilled in his little pulsating scarlet throat was mine. He sang it only to me—and he would never sing it when any one else was there to hear. When we were quite alone with only roses and bees and sunshine and silence about us, when he swung on some spray quite close to me and I stood and talked to him in whispers—then he would answer me—each time I paused—with the little "far away" sounding trills—the sweetest, most wonderful little sounds in the world. A clever person who knew more of the habits of birds than I did told me a most curious thing.

"That is his little mating song," he said. "You have inspired a hopeless passion in a robin."

Perhaps so. He thought the rose-garden was the world and it seemed to me he never went out of it during the summer months. At whatsoever hour I appeared and called him he came out of bushes but from a different point each time. In late autumn however, one afternoon I *saw* him fly to me from over a wall dividing the enclosed garden from the open ones. I thought he looked guilty and fluttered when he alighted near me. I think he did not want me to know.

The Robin at rest among the silk roses on Frances's hat.

"You have been making the acquaintance of a young lady robin," I said to him. "Perhaps you are already engaged to her for the next season."

He tried to persuade me that it was not true but I felt he was not entirely frank.

After that it was plain that he had discovered that the rose-garden was not *all* the world. He knew about the other side of the wall. But it did not absorb him altogether. He was seldom absent when I came and he never failed to answer my call. I talked to him often about the young lady robin but though he showed a gentle-manly reticence on the subject I knew quite well he loved me best. He loved my robin sounds, he loved my whispers, his dewy dark eyes looked into mine as if he knew we two understood strange tender things others did not.

I was only a mere tenant of the beautiful place I had had for nine years and that winter the owner sold the estate. In December I was to go to Montreux for a couple of months; in March I was to return to Maytham and close it before leaving it finally. Until I left for Switzerland I saw my robin every day. Before I went away I called him to me and told him where I was going.

He was such a little thing. Two or three months might seem a lifetime to him. He might not remember me so long. I was not a real robin. I was only a human being. I said a great many things to him—wondering if he would even be in the garden when I came back. I went away wondering.

When I returned from the world of winter sports, of mountain snows, of tobogganing and skis I felt as if I had been absent a long time. There had been snow even in Kent and the park and gardens were white. I arrived in the evening. The next morning I threw on my red frieze garden cloak and went down the flagged terrace and the Long Walk through the walled gardens to the beloved place where the rose bushes stood dark and slender and leafless among the whiteness. I went to my own tree and stood under it and called.

"Are you gone," I said in my heart; "are you gone, little Soul? Shall I never see you again?"

251

After the call I waited—and I had never waited before. The roses were gone and he was not in the rose-world. I called again. The call was sometimes a soft whistle as near a robin sound as I could make it—sometimes it was a chirp—sometimes it was a quick clear repetition of "Sweet! Sweet! Sweetie"—which I fancied he liked best. I made one after the other—and then—something scarlet flashed across the lawn, across the rose-walk—over the wall and he was there. He had not forgotten, it had not been too long, he alighted on the snowy brown grass at my feet.

Then I knew he was a little Soul and not only a bird and the real parting which must come in a few weeks' time loomed up before me a strange tragic thing.

. . . .

I do not often allow myself to think of it. It was too final. And there was nothing to be done. I was going thousands of miles across the sea. A little warm thing of scarlet and brown feathers and pulsating trilling throat lives such a brief life. The little soul in its black dew-drop eye—one knows nothing about it. For myself I sometimes believe strange things. We two were something weirdly near to each other.

At the end I went down to the bare world of roses one soft damp day and stood under the tree and called him for the last time. He did not keep me waiting and he flew to a twig very near my face. I could not write all I said to him. I tried with all my heart to explain and he answered me—between his listenings—with the "far away" love note. I talked to him as if he knew all I knew. He put his head on one side and listened so intently that I felt that he understood. I told him that I must go away and that we should not see each other again and I told him why.

"But you must not think when I do not come back it is because I have forgotten you," I said. "Never since I was born have I loved anything as I have loved you—except my two babies. Never shall I love anything so much again so long as I am in the world. You are a little Soul and I am a little Soul and we shall love each other forever and ever. We won't say Goodbye. We have been too near to each other—nearer than human beings are. I love you and love you and love you—little Soul."

Then I went out of the rose-garden. I shall never go into it again.

IN THE GARDEN

FRANCES HODGSON BURNETT

The anonymously illustrated cover to Burnett's *In the Garden*.

GARDENING FOR EVERYBODY:
IN THE GARDEN
(1924)

In 1904, Burnett interrupted an interviewer. "Can't we talk about gardens?" she asked. "I love them." Then she predicted, "I'm going to write a garden book someday." It took her twenty years to fulfill her pledge, and she did not live to see it in print. She had gotten an assignment from *The Country Gentleman*, a popular magazine, for a series of six gardening essays called "Gardening for Everybody." She began as her health was failing. After her death, Vivian brought the manuscript of the one extended piece she had finished to a publisher. In a sense, this short book is both gardening memoir and her bequest to the rest of us.

Vivian drew the book's title from the concluding chapter of *The Secret Garden*. It was fitting. Just as the spirit of Lilias Craven had whispered "in the garden" to her husband to draw him back to their son, Burnett's final work leaves us with a message to carry forward. Garden where you are. Garden with what you have. Simply garden.

IN THE GARDEN

BY FRANCES HODGSON BURNETT

I AM WRITING IN the garden. To write as one should of a garden one must not write outside it or merely somewhere near it, but in the garden.

All my life I have been a passionate gardener—since I was seven years old and hung over a border of small flowers I do not now know the name of, which tiny long-remembered things grew round a small bed in the centre of the few yards of iron-railed front garden before a house in an old square in the ugliest, smokiest factory town to be found anywhere in all the North of England.

I have lived a thousand years since then, but I still feel them— the little pink and blue and white creatures who had the courage and determination to force themselves through the soot-soaked soil and boldly live surrounded by the tall factory chimneys pouring forth smoke which tarnished even the white clouds and blue sky.

I wonder what they were.

I have had many gardens in many countries, but I have not seen them since.

Wheresoever I go I can never leave the earth alone. I must make some bit of it into a garden while I am near it.

I have made gardens in queer places. If that were not quite another story it would be amusing to relate the history of how gardens can be made to spring up in places where they are horribly wanted—not large gardens and not through spending much money. But still gardens.

As long as one has a garden one has a future; and as long as one has a future one is alive. It is remaining alive which makes life worth living—not merely remaining on the surface of the earth. And it is the looking forward to a future which makes the difference between the two states of being.

There are a number of things and conditions which will provide futures if time and interest are given to them, but no one of them seems so natural, so simple and so alluring as making a garden.

To the gardener in winter one's future is the spring. All the dark months may be filled by it.

To live in brilliantly colored and eloquent catalogues is to dream dreams unlike all others that glorify our days; to pore over gardening books is to glow with joy, ambition and flaming desire for loveliness, color, fragrance and still, sweet delight.

In the spring, which is the future of the darkest winter days, the garden one's imagination sees is carpeted in its first hours with crocuses and dazzling blue scillas, golden cushions and borders of alyssum saxatile, purple mats of aubrietia; in its second hours daffodils and jonquils fill every corner and are only crowded out by white narcissuses and tulips of every shade of scarlet and white, and iris of every tint of yellow and violet and lavender and blue, with azalea bushes flaming coral or thrilling rose here and there behind or between.

The summer, which is to be the future of the spring, finds one almost reeling before its first outburst of roses of all blushes and pallors and sunlight—yellows and crimsons—and carries on with the blues and violets and flushed turquoise of delphiniums and the splendors of every other shade and color in the world.

The autumn is a flare of golden trumpets singing in all-brilliant tones the triumph of the past year and heralding the future of the spring for which the winter will prepare.

As long as one has a garden one has a future, and as long as one has a future one is alive.

If while living in one's own garden one could simply relate day by day the things which happen in it, the things which happen to it, the things which happen to the gardener! What a human document the record would end by becoming! What a revelation of one's power to imagine and one's determination to create! Also, if it were done faithfully, how practical and useful it would be!

It is only personal experience which provides actual facts and information.

The daily story should be told faithfully and in simple phrases. And the gardener should be of a gay and valiant spirit. How can it be possible to complain of a garden or a flower?

It need not be a large garden which provides the daily record. The smallest patch of earth will serve.

To plant a packet of seeds, whether in a greenhouse in March or in a garden bed in May; to water them with the proper delicacy and restraint; to watch until the first tiny ghost of a leaf pushes aside the soil; to cry out with joy at the sight of it and then perhaps to discover that it is only a weed; to wait again, to wait longer than you thought you must wait; then after coming again and again and finding nothing, to arrive one day to see a small thrusting leaf once more, and then not one but another and another and at last a whole regiment of small valiant green soldiers marching in a row all crying aloud, "We are alive! We have come from the Outside into the Garden! We are here—here!

Oh, well! There is a thrill in it, and one never gets over the sense of the mystery and the wonder. That is always new and startling as the spring is.

First just the tiny seeds—little black things—twenty-five cents a packet; then the breathless waiting while the soft, silent, black earth seems to be doing nothing. Then under the black earth slow, soft, unseen stirring. And then suddenly out of the darkness leaps life—life!

I have a theory that every one in the world really wants a garden, though many perhaps are not conscious of their need. There are thousands and thousands of women, and it may be as many men, who know they want to work in the earth and breathe the sweet damp scent of it and make things grow, but they think it is not possible for them to do it.

They think their bit of earth, their small back yard or front yard, is too small or too sandy or too shady. But nothing is too small to grow a flower—nothing is too sandy to be enriched and made fertile. Shade is the greatest obstacle to bloom, but there are ferns which grow in the shade and a number of things which will even bloom in it, if it is not of the darkness of a cellar.

And I am speaking to the thousands of people who are living on farms or in country places where, to quote Lavengro:

"Life is sweet, brother! There's day and night, brother! both sweet things; sun, moon and stars, brother! all sweet things: There is likewise a wind on the heath."

One cannot murmur words like these to oneself when one lives in great cities where life is rank with the stench of petrol, day and night are roaring pandemonium, and sun, moon and stars seem not to belong to the system of things in which one is conscious only of smells and increasing uproar and the crowding of human bodies crushing past each other, while on all sides machinery drills and hammers, tearing down walls and roofs, reducing structures which once were homes to masses of bricks and mortar and flying clouds of dust.

Sitting under my special oak tree in my garden—it is always spoken of merely as "the tree," though there are a hundred others—I like to think of the thousands of women and girls and children to whom I may be saying:

"In your heart of hearts you really want a garden. You can have one. You can make it yourself. Anyone can have a garden—if it is only two yards wide. I say this because I know. If you can only love a large garden then you will need money, gardeners, hotbeds and cold frames and greenhouses, but if your heart longs only for a garden and you are willing to plan for it, care for it, love it, you can have one."

I have always felt on reading gardening books and articles in gardening magazines that I learned the most from the woman who said, "I planted this flower in this way," or, "I planned the colors in this corner to produce this effect," or, "This flower was beautiful but did not bloom long enough to be worth the trouble and money it cost."

When I read this I knew that I had learned something from actual experience, though it was not my own, but the experience of another person.

It is as a result of this that when I say, "You can have a garden if you want one," I can only go on to tell you a very few practical things I have found out myself in making gardens for myself and in superintending various incompetent but expensive people I was obliged to call in to do the work I was too busy or not well enough to do.

I should always have preferred to have been at least two strong men in one and to have done all the work with my own hands.

I love it all. I love to dig. I love to kneel down on the grass at the edge of a flower bed and pull out the weeds fiercely and throw them into a heap by my side. I love to fight with those who can spring up again almost in a night and taunt me. I tear them up by the roots again and again, and when at last after many days, perhaps, it seems as if I have beaten them for a time at least, I go away feeling like an army with banners.

I really try to keep my rule that I will not allow myself to hate anything on earth, but I am afraid that I absolutely know what hate is when I come upon a dozen flaunting ragweeds which while my back was turned have sprung up in a bed of lovely, tender, colored snapdragons, trying to pretend that they are only part of their foliage.

Then, while I take them out by the roots—carefully, lest I disturb a lovely young snapdragon—it is necessary for me to control evil impulses which I should prefer to believe did not lurk in the depths of an apparently mild nature.

Pusley is worse. It is more sneaking and creeping, and I do believe more rapid. I prefer not to speak of pusley.

When I say that I love all the work in the garden I am not discriminating. One of the loveliest dreams of my life is my memory of a softly rainy spring in Kent when I spent nearly three weeks kneeling on a small rubber mat on the grass edge of a heavenly old herbaceous border bed, which a big young gardener was trenching and remaking, while I followed him and tucked softly into the rich sweet damp mold the plants which were to bloom in loveliness for me in the summer.

The rain was not constant. It only softly drizzled in a sort of mist on my red frieze garden cloak and hood.

The bed was on one side of what was called The Long Walk. At the back of it was an ancient buttressed brick wall hidden by ivy and espalier fruit trees with their branches trained to lie flat against the old bricks. On the other side, behind me, was a high clipped laurel hedge where nests were being built. Beyond that were spreading velvet lawns embracing flower beds and great trees.

And day after day I knelt on the grass edge and tucked my plants into the dark rich mellow English earth. And oh, the scent of it! And the gray soft mist floating about one! And the fluting of birds in the wide boughed trees, and the little cries and darting by of wings which sometimes seemed almost to touch one's cheek as they passed! How could they be forgotten?

One useful discovery I have made in years of planning and watching flower beds. And I have only reached my decisions concerning it during the last few years.

It is a realization of the value of some very simple and old-fashioned flowers which used to be so common that you have known them all your lives, and so have your grandmothers, and have regarded them with a certain disdain as mere country cousins scarcely worth planting.

People are always overpraising and overestimating my garden. They insist that it is wonderful—which it is not at all. When they enter it they cry out, "Oh, what a beautiful garden; I never saw such flowers! I never saw such a garden!"

And they will not believe me when I say, "My dears, it is all camouflage. There are no rare flowers in it at all. It is filled with the most ordinary things you can buy in fifteen and twenty cent packages.

"But it looks beautiful because it is full of flowers. And it is full because I will have them, and I plant big groups of them together, and I use a great deal of white in masses because it throws up and makes more brilliant any color it is near. And I will not give room to things which have a brief blooming, because I cannot afford the time. This garden must look as if it were full of color until the end of November and later—by the grace of God."

And then I tell them what the faithful things are which I have discovered will bloom for me all the summer and all the autumn and until frost comes, some wonders even defying frosts, if they are not too severe.

Of course the people I am speaking of are not expert gardeners or they would know more than I do. There are, I find, about four expert and two passionate gardeners in a million people. All the million "like flowers," but most of them do not know the simplest by name. So I explain to them how common in variety most of my loveliest and most decorative masses of color are.

"The flowers they are made of used to be in farmhouse back gardens. Most of them at that time were of ugly magenta reds and pinks. They were the old-fashioned petunias and stiff zinnias which were almost invariably of hideous flaring colors. Expert hybridizing has developed their size and given us new varieties with all the old farmyard hardiness, but of exquisite tints and shades.

The flower beds that Frances loved were packed with color,
with the exception of "ugly magenta reds and pinks."

"That bed at the side of the wall which looks like a fairy heap
of pink rose petals is nothing but a bed of Rosy Morn petunias. The
heap of snow you see behind the roses is Snowball petunia, which is
soft and double and pure white. The border of this little formal garden is made of single whites mixed with Purple Queen.

"That tropical splendid mass of orange surrounded by tall
ferny green is nothing more than a planting of Orange King African

marigold put among things which are ceasing to bloom. Those magnificent tall flames of scarlet and yellow and crimson which you may think are dahlias are the great new zinnias which are many of them quite as large as any ordinary dahlia bloom."

I give them a hundred proofs that the flowers are neither rare nor marvelous, but still because of its masses of bloom they always go away saying, "The garden is wonderful!"

I do not mean to say that I have spent no money on my garden and that it contains nothing but petunias and zinnias and marigolds. That would be misleading. It is only a little garden of three acres. It is on a pretty bay on Long Island, which makes it look much larger than it is.

I have planted a great many shrubs in it and enclosed it with trees and high trimmed hedges. I have also a great many roses and divers other things, but I am really writing this to assure those who see the practical side of things that if I had not found out by experience the modern beauty of color, the floriferous abundance and the lasting faithful blooming of mere petunias, zinnias, marigolds and single hardy chrysanthemums, there would be many times during the seasons when the kind people who overpraise my garden would come into it to find bare places instead of masses of rose and pink and white and velvet purple and flame, and they would not always cry out to me, "The garden is wonderful!"

Moreover, if I had a bit of ground at the front of a farmhouse or cottage on a country road—or anywhere—if I wanted a garden there I should get a flower catalogue or so and look up the colors of

annuals which are bounteous enough to go on blooming and blooming all through the summer and autumn, and I should make my bit of
ground soft and rich and black, and dream about my colors while I
was working, and plant seeds and take care of them until the miracle
happened at its appointed time and I could sit upon my porch and
watch waving snow white and rose and violet velvet and peach pink,
and wonder and plan the next spring's planting.

It is true. I have seen it. That is why I say if you want a garden
you can have it.

And as long as you have a garden you have a future, and as long
as you have a future you are alive.

The rose from Frances Hodgson's childhood alphabet book.

EIGHT

FRANCES'S PLANTS

AN ANNOTATED LIST

Of course I know that I am flower drunk.
I want millions & I want them always—
Spring, Summer, Autumn, & Winter—
particularly Winter.

—From a letter to Elizabeth Jordan, June 1922

65. Primulaceae

1:1. *Primula vulgaris*
Primrose.

Douglas June 10 '94

One of the wildflowers that Frances appreciated was the spring-blooming
English primrose, illustrated by Helen Sharp.

O NE REASON MY garden beds are so crowded is that I read too much. Whenever I start researching a new author-gardener, I always want to try some of the plants they grew, especially the ones that also have appeared in their books.

To create Frances Hodgson Burnett's plant inventory, I decided to focus on *The Secret Garden* and her gardens at Maytham Hall, Plandome Park, and Clifton Heights. Unfortunately, Frances didn't catalogue her gardens in a systematic way. Or if she did, the lists didn't survive. I've combed her correspondence and nonfiction writings, plus accounts by reliable visitors to create this list, which is in alphabetical order by common name. In *The Secret Garden*, Colin and Mary show Dickon pictures of flowers in a gardening book. Dickon says in his broad Yorkshire, "I couldna' say that there name," pointing to one labeled *Aquilegia*, "but us calls that a columbine, an' that there one it's a snapdragon and they both grow wild in hedges, but these is garden ones an' they're bigger an' grander." I have made the assumption that if "columbine" was good enough for Dickon, it was good enough for Burnett as well, though she did refer to snapdragons as "antirrhinums."

You will find mostly ornamentals—flowering shrubs, perennials, and annuals. I've included fruit but have omitted vegetables. While her letters itemize the fruits growing in her garden, there are few mentions of vegetables except in connection with her son, who grew peas, potatoes, and rhubarb in the aforementioned Sneak Garden on the property they shared at Plandome Park. I should add that fictional potatoes, onions, cabbages, radishes, turnips, and parsley appear in *The Secret Garden* in connection with Ben Weatherstaff and Dickon Sowerby. My suspicion is that Burnett felt that vegetable growing was something one left to the men.

Wildflowers rarely appear in her correspondence with the exception of a few ecstatic letters to Vivian from the Alps, though she did take note of the wild primroses, bluebells, and anemones at Maytham Hall. While amateur naturalists abounded at the time, Burnett wasn't one of them, and gardeners weren't much interested in native plants for their ornamental beds until later in the twentieth century. In *The Secret Garden*, Burnett stretched her descriptive powers to include the plants of the moorland, so you will also find a handful of wildflowers in the list.

The following abbreviations are used in this table and/or in "Sources and Citations."

PROPER NAMES

EF	Edith Hodgson Fahnestock Jordan, her sister and close companion.
EJ	Elizabeth Jordan, her intimate friend in later life.
FBJ	Frances Benjamin Johnson, photographer, photo CL352-1202, Huntington Library.
MFR	Mary Fanton Roberts, acquaintance and author of "Mrs. Burnett's Rose Garden in Kent," *The Craftsman*, August 1907.
RWG	Richard Watson Gilder, her mentor and editor at Scribner's.
VB	Vivian Burnett, her younger and only surviving son.

WORKS BY FRANCES HODGSON BURNETT

Ha-ha "An American Author's English Ha-ha," *Country Life in America,* July 1906.

ITG *In the Garden,* Philadelphia: Curtis Publishing Company, 1924, and Boston: The Medici Society of America, 1925.

MR *My Robin,* New York: Frederick A. Stokes Company, 1912.

TOI *The One I Knew the Best of All,* New York: Charles Scribner's Sons, 1893.

TSG *The Secret Garden,* New York: Frederick A. Stokes Company, 1911.

WORKS ABOUT FRANCES HODGSON BURNETT

GER Gerzina, Gretchen. *Frances Hodgson Burnett: The Unpredictable Life of the Author of The Secret Garden,* London: Chatto & Windus, 2004.

HAE Burnett, Constance Buel. *Happily Ever After: A Portrait of Frances Hodgson Burnett,* New York: Vanguard Press, 1969.

SMN Burnett, Vivian. *A Story Maker's Notes By the Way,* undated manuscript in Princeton University Library, Manuscripts Division, Department of Special Collections.

TRL Burnett, Vivian. *The Romantick Lady: The Life Story of an Imagination,* New York: Charles Scribner's Sons, 1927.

WFP Thwaite, Ann. *Waiting for the Party,* Boston: David R. Godine, 1991.

ARCHIVAL SOURCES

NYPL New York Public Library, Elizabeth Jordan Collection, Manuscripts and Archives Division.

PUL Princeton University Library, Manuscripts Division, Department of Special Collections (unless otherwise noted, material is from the Vivian Burnett Collection of Frances Hodgson Burnett, C1304); Cotsen Children's Library, Department of Special Collections.

COMMON NAME	SCIENTIFIC NAME	TYPE	LETTERS ET AL.	MAYTHAM HALL	PLANDOME PARK	CLIFTON HEIGHTS	TSG
African daisy	*Arctotis ×hybrida*	annual	From VB, 17 Mar 1911		X		
ageratum	*Ageratum houstonianum*	annual	To EJ, 26 Jun 1922; from EF, undated		X	X	
almond, flowering	*Prunus glandulosa*	shrub	From VB, late Mar 1911		X		
alyssum	*Lobularia maritima*	annual	From VB, 10 May 1912		X		
amaryllis	*Hippeastrum*	perennial	To VB, 5 May 1921			X	
anchusa	*Anchusa azurea*	annual	To VB, [1911?]		X		
anemone	*Anemone coronaria*	perennial	To EF, undated; to VB, 5 May 1921	X		X	
—St. Brigid	*A. c.* 'St. Brigid'	annual	To VB, 5 May 1921			X	
anemone, wood	*Anemone nemorosa*	perennial	To EF, 2 May 1899	X			
apple	*Malus domestica*	fruit	To VB, 22 Jul 1898	X			Chapters 15, 16, 21
aster, China	*Callistephus chinensis*	annual	From VB, 17 Mar 1911		X		
aubrietia	*Aubrieta deltoidea*	perennial	ITG p. 28		X		
aurantiaca	*Gynura aurantiaca*	annual	From VB, late Mar 1911		X		
azalea	*Rhododendron*	shrub	To EF, 2 May 1899; from VB, 29 May 1912	X	X		
baby's breath	*Gypsophila*	annual	To EJ, undated		X		

COMMON NAME	SCIENTIFIC NAME	TYPE	LETTERS ET AL.	MAYTHAM HALL	PLANDOME PARK	CLIFTON HEIGHTS	TSG
balloon flower	*Platycodon*	perennial	To VB, 9 Feb 1913		X		
begonia	*Begonia* 'Gloire de Lorraine'	annual	To VB, 21 Feb 1913		X		
blackberry	*Rubus fruticosus*	fruit					Chapter 4
black-eyed susan	*Rudbeckia*	perennial	To VB, [1911?]		X		
—Autumn Sun	*Rudbeckia* 'Herbstsonne'	perennial	To VB, [1911?]		X		
bluebell	*Hyacinthoides non-scripta*	perennial	To VB, 22 Jul 1898	X			
blue lace flower	*Trachymene coerulea*	annual	To VB, 4 Apr 1921			X	
broom	*Cytisus scoparius*	perennial					Chapters 3, 4, 7
campanula	*Campanula*	perennial					Chapters 11, 23
candytuft	*Iberis sempervirens*	perennial	To VB, 5 May 1921			X	
canna	*Canna*	perennial	From VB, 10 Apr 1911; to VB, 5 May 1921		X	X	
Canterbury bells	*Campanula medium*	annual	To EJ, 30 Jun 1924		X		Chapter 11
Cape marigold	*Dimorphotheca sinuata*	annual	From VB, late Mar 1911		X		
catalpa	*Catalpa bignonioides*	tree	From VB, mid-Mar 1912		X		
cherry	*Prunus avium*	fruit	To VB, 22 Jul 1898; from VB, 10 Apr 1911	X	X		Chapters 16, 21
chestnut	*Castanea sativa*	tree	To VB, 22 Jul 1898	X			
chrysanthemum, hardy	*Chrysanthemum*	perennial	To VB, 1 Jun 1920		X		
clematis	*Clematis*	vine	To EF, 2 May 1899	X			

COMMON NAME	SCIENTIFIC NAME	TYPE	LETTERS ET AL.	MAYTHAM HALL	PLANDOME PARK	CLIFTON HEIGHTS	TSG
columbine	*Aquilegia*	perennial	From VB, 1 Jun 1920		X		Chapters 19, 23
copperleaf	*Acalypha wilkesiana*	perennial	To VB, 25 Feb 1912			X	
coreopsis	*Coreopsis*	perennial	To VB, 5 May 1921			X	
cornflower	*Centaurea cyanus*	annual	From EF, undated			X	
cosmos	*Cosmos bipinnatus*	annual	From VB, 17 Mar 1911	X			
crocus	*Crocus*	perennial	To EF, undated	X			Chapters 7, 9, 15, 17, 22
croton	*Codiaeum variegatum*	perennial	To VB, 25 Feb 1912			X	
currant	*Ribes*	shrub	To VB, 22 Jul 1898	X			Chapter 10
daffodil	*Narcissus*	perennial	To EF, 2 May 1899; from VB, 10 Apr 1911	X	X		Chapters 7, 9, 13, 17
daffodil, jonquil	*Narcissus jonquilla*	perennial	Ha-ha	X			
daffodil, poet's	*Narcissus poeticus*	perennial	Ha-ha	X			
dahlia	*Dahlia*	annual	From VB, 10 Apr 1911; to VB, 5 May 1921	X	X	X	
delphinium	*Delphinium*	perennial	From VB, 1 May 1912		X		Chapters 19, 23
elephant ears	*Colocasia*	perennial	From EF, 1914			X	
fig	*Ficus carica*	tree	To VB, 22 Jul 1898	X			
forget-me-not	*Myosotis*	biennial					Chapter 27
forsythia	*Forsythia ×intermedia*	shrub	From VB, late Mar 1911		X		

COMMON NAME	SCIENTIFIC NAME	TYPE	LETTERS ET AL.	MAYTHAM HALL	PLANDOME PARK	CLIFTON HEIGHTS	TSG
foxglove	*Digitalis purpurea*	biennial					Chapter 24
gentian	*Gentiana*	perennial	To VB, Jun 1910		X		Chapter 27
geranium	*Pelargonium*	annual	To EJ, undated		X		
gladiola	*Gladiolus*	annual	From VB, 10 Apr 1911		X		
gooseberry	*Ribes uva-crispa*	shrub	To VB, 22 Jul 1898	X			Chapter 24
gorse	*Ulex europaeus*	perennial					Chapters 3, 7, 14, 19, 20, 24
grape	*Vitis vinifera*	vine	To VB, 22 Jul 1898	X			
hawthorn	*Crataegus monogyna*	tree	To VB, 5 Jun 1898; from VB, 29 May 1912	X	X		
hazelnut	*Corylus avellana*	shrub	To VB, 22 Jul 1898	X			
heather	*Calluna vulgaris*	perennial					Chapters 3, 4, 7, 15, 24, 26
heliotrope	*Heliotropium arborescens*	annual	From VB, late Mar 1911; from EF, undated		X	X	
hibiscus	*Hibiscus rosa-sinensis*	shrub	To VB, 23 Jan 1912			X	Chapter 1
holly	*Ilex*	tree	To EF, 30 Sep 1899	X			Chapter 10
hollyhock	*Alcea rosea*	annual	SMN p. 14–9		X		
horse-chestnut, red	*Aesculus ×carnea*	tree	To VB, 5 Jun 1898	X			
hyacinth	*Hyacinthus orientalis*	perennial	To EF, 2 May 1899; from VB, 10 Apr 1911	X	X		

COMMON NAME	SCIENTIFIC NAME	TYPE	LETTERS ET AL.	MAYTHAM HALL	PLANDOME PARK	CLIFTON HEIGHTS	TSG
iris	Iris	perennial	To EF, undated; from VB, 29 May 1912	X	X		Chapters 9, 17, 23
ivy	Hedera helix	vine	To VB, 24 Jun 1906	X			Chapters 4, 5, 7–11, 13, 18, 20, 27
jasmine	Jasminum	vine	To EF, 2 May 1899	X			
laburnum	Laburnum anagyroides	tree	To VB, 31 May 1905	X			
larkspur	Consolida ajacis	annual	To VB, 9 Feb 1913; to VB, 26 Apr 1916		X	X	Chapters 10, 19
laurel	Prunus laurocerasus	shrub	To EF, 2 May 1899	X			Chapters 10, 27
lilac	Syringa vulgaris	shrub	To VB, 31 May 1905; from VB, 19 Apr 1912	X	X		Chapter 20
lily	Lilium	perennial	To VB, 30 Sep 1899; to VB, [1911?]	X	X		Chapters 9, 13, 17, 23, 27
lily-of-the-valley	Convallaria majalis	perennial					Chapter 11
lobelia	Lobelia erinus	annual	From VB, 17 Mar 1911		X		
love-in-a-mist	Nigella damascena	annual	From VB, 10 Apr 1911; to VB, [1911?]		X	X	
lupine	Lupinus ×hybrida	perennial	To VB, 24 Jun 1906	X			
marigold	Tagetes	annual	ITG p. 28		X		Chapters 2, 11
—Orange King	Tagetes 'Orange King'	annual	ITG p. 28		X		
Mexican fireweed	Bassia scoparia*	annual	From VB, 10 Apr 1911		X		

*Now considered invasive in much of North America

COMMON NAME	SCIENTIFIC NAME	TYPE	LETTERS ET AL.	MAYTHAM HALL	PLANDOME PARK	CLIFTON HEIGHTS	TSG
mignonette	Reseda odorata	annual	To VB, 24 Mar 1921		X		Chapters 10, 24
nasturtium	Tropaeolum majus	annual	FBJ; to VB, 9 Feb 1913	X	X		
nectarine	Prunus persica var. nucipersica	tree	To VB, 22 Jul 1898	X			
oak	Quercus	tree	SMN p. 14–8		X		Chapter 20
oleander	Nerium oleander	shrub	To VB, 26 Apr 1916			X	
ostrich plume	Alpinia purpurata	annual	To VB, [1911?]		X		
pansy	Viola	annual					Chapter 24
peach	Prunus persica	tree	To VB, 22 Jul 1898; from VB, 1 May 1912	X	X		Chapter 16
pear	Pyrus communis	vine	To VB, 22 Jul 1898	X			
penstemon	Penstemon	annual	To VB, 2 May 1921			X	
peony	Paeonia lactiflora	perennial	To EJ, undated		X		
peony, tree	Paeonia ×suffruticosa	shrub	From VB, late Mar 1911		X		
Peruvian lily	Alstroemeria	perennial	To VB, [1911?]		X		
petunia	Petunia ×atkinsiana	annual	ITG p. 27; to VB, 5 May 1921		X	X	
petunia cvs	'Purple Queen', 'Rosy Morn', 'Snowball'	annual	ITG pp. 27–28		X		
phlox	Phlox paniculata	perennial	Ha-ha	X			
phlox, annual	Phlox drummondii	annual	To VB, 9 Feb 1913		X		
pink	Dianthus	annual					Chapter 24

COMMON NAME	SCIENTIFIC NAME	TYPE	LETTERS ET AL.	MAYTHAM HALL	PLANDOME PARK	CLIFTON HEIGHTS	TSG
plum	*Prunus domestica*	fruit					Chapters 16, 21, 24
poppy	*Papaver*	annual	To VB, 24 Jun 1906; from VB, 17 Mar 1911; from EF, undated	X	X	X	Chapters 10, 23
poppy, Oriental	*Papaver orientale*	perennial	To EJ, undated		X		
primrose	*Primula vulgaris*	perennial	To VB, 5 Jun 1898	X			Chapter 19
privet	*Ligustrum vulgare*	shrub	From VB, 1 May 1912		X		
pyrethrum	*Tanacetum coccineum*	annual	To VB, [1911?]		X		
quince, flowering	*Chaenomeles speciosa*	shrub	From VB, 1 May 1912		X		
rhododendron	*Rhododendron*	shrub	To EF, 2 May 1899; from VB, 29 May 1912	X	X		Chapter 21
rose	*Rosa*	shrub		X	X	X	Chapters 4, 5, 7–14, 16–17, 19, 22–24, 26–27
—Agrippina	*Rosa* 'Cramoisi Supérieur'	shrub	To VB, 23 Jan 1912			X	
—Cora	*Rosa* 'Cora'	shrub	MFR p. 547	X			
—Dean Hole	*Rosa* 'Dean Hole'	shrub	From VB, 1 May 1912		X		
—Ducher	*Rosa* 'Ducher'	shrub	MFR p. 538	X			
—Duke of Connaught	*Rosa* 'Duke of Connaught'	shrub	MFR p. 547	X			
—Frau Karl Druschki	*Rosa* 'Frau Karl Druschki'	shrub	To VB, undated; to VB 28 Dec 1911		X	X	
—Golden Glow	*Rosa* 'Golden Glow'	shrub	To VB, undated		X		

Common Name	Scientific Name	Type	Letters et al.	Maytham Hall	Plandome Park	Clifton Heights	TSG
—Gruss an Teplitz	*Rosa* 'Gruss an Teplitz'	shrub	From VB, 1 May 1912		X		
—Louis Philippe	*Rosa* 'Louis Philippe'	shrub	MFR p. 547	X			
—Lyon	*Rosa* 'Lyon'	shrub	From VB, 1 May 1912		X		
—Madame Kesal	*Rosa* 'Madame Kesal'	shrub	MFR p. 546	X			
—Madame Laurette Messimy	*Rosa* 'Madame Laurette Messimy'	shrub	MR p. 19	X			
—Maman Cochet	*Rosa* 'Maman Cochet'	shrub	MFR p. 545	X			
—Melody	*Rosa* 'Melody'	shrub	From VB, 10 May 1912		X		
—Paul Neyron	*Rosa* 'Paul Neyron'	shrub	MFR p. 538	X			
—Paul's Carmine Pillar	*Rosa* 'Paul's Carmine Pillar'	shrub	MFR p. 545	X			
—Prince Arthur	*Rosa* 'Prince Arthur'	shrub	MFR p. 547	X			
—Red Radiance	*Rosa* 'Red Radiance'	shrub	To VB, 12 May 1920		X		
—Sunburst	*Rosa* 'Sunburst'	shrub	From VB, 10 May 1912		X		
—Viscountess Folkestone	*Rosa* 'Viscountess Folkestone'	shrub	MFR p. 547	X			
rose, wichuraiana	*Rosa wichuraiana*	shrub	MFR p. 547	X			
salpiglossis	*Salpiglossis sinuata*	annual	From VB, 17 Mar 1911		X		
salvia	*Salvia*	annual	From VB, 10 May 1912		X		
Shasta daisy	*Leucanthemum ×superbum*	perennial	To VB, [1911?]		X		
snapdragon	*Antirrhinum majus*	annual	To EJ, 26 Jun 1922; to VB, 26 Apr 1916		X	X	Chapter 19

Frances looks for the robin, standing at the wall of her rose garden at Maytham Hall.

COMMON NAME	SCIENTIFIC NAME	TYPE	LETTERS ET AL.	MAYTHAM HALL	PLANDOME PARK	CLIFTON HEIGHTS	TSG
—Orange Beauty	A. m. 'Orange Beauty'	annual	To VB, 26 Apr 1916		X	X	
snowdrop	Galanthus nivalis	perennial	To EF, undated	X			Chapters 7, 9, 10, 13, 17
sour orange	Citrus ×aurantium	perennial	To VB, 25 Feb 1912			X	
spirea	Spiraea	shrub	From VB, mid-Mar 1912		X		
squill	Scilla siberica	perennial	From VB, late Mar 1911		X		
strawberry	Fragaria ×ananassa	fruit	To VB, 22 Jul 1898	X			
sunflower	Helianthus annuus	annual	To VB, 2 May 1921			X	
sweet pea	Lathyrus odoratus	annual	Ha-ha; from VB, 10 Apr 1911; to VB, 29 Nov 1920	X	X	X	
tulip	Tulipa	perennial	To EF, 2 May 1899; from VB, 29 May 1912	X	X		
verbena	Verbena	annual	From VB, 10 May 1912		X		
wallflower	Erysimum cheiri	annual	To RWG, 10 May 1910	X			
walnut, English	Juglans regia	tree	To VB, 22 Jul 1898	X			
wandering jew	Tradescantia	perennial	From EF, undated			X	
water lily	Nymphaea	perennial	To EJ, undated		X		
weigela	Weigela florida	shrub	To VB, 23 Jan 1912; from VB, 29 May 1912		X	X	
wisteria	Wisteria sinensis	vine	From VB, 16 Jun 1916		X		
zinnia	Zinnia elegans	annual	ITG p. 28		X		

Frances Hodgson Burnett in 1881.

SOWING SEEDS

BY KERI WILT, FRANCES HODGSON BURNETT'S GREAT-GREAT-GRANDDAUGHTER

And the secret garden bloomed and bloomed
and every morning revealed new miracles.

—*The Secret Garden*

MORNING MIRACLES HAVE been happening in our family for over 150 years. They can all be traced back to the seeds that each generation has chosen to sow.

My great-great-grandmother Frances was a seed planter long before she ever had a garden of her own. She planted her words on paper so that readers could be entertained. She planted joy in the hearts of orphan boys on Drury Lane in London by building a library for them. She even planted courage in her son as he died of tuberculosis, so he would not be afraid of death. And she planted happy endings so that others might believe in them too.

Whether we can keep a houseplant alive or not, the seeds we plant with our words and actions have the power to make things come alive in generations to come. What will you choose to plant? Kindness, encouraging words, a garden?

In *The Secret Garden* Mary asks Dickon, "Will you show the seeds to me?" Actual gardening can be intimidating, so let me give you some hope if you have been holding out. Our family's love of gardening was not the result of kneeling side by side with the previous generation with our hands in the dirt. It was born through the observation of the happiness that a garden creates. Each generation of our family learned to love and tend gardens by mimicking what we saw.

Frances didn't physically teach me, her granddaughters, or her son Vivian how to garden. All she did was plant and water the seeds in her own backyard. Just as Mary muses in *The Secret Garden*, it seems that Frances thought, "If I had a little spade I could dig somewhere… and I might make a little garden." The simple act of sowing seeds and the blooms that followed inspired her son to grow good things too. What he planted went on to inspire his daughter Verity, whose blooms delighted her daughter, whose blossoms continue to inspire me.

My mother never put me to work in her garden either, but she planted the seed by simply showing me the joy it brought her. It was reflected in the kitchen table pitcher that overflowed with her weekly floral bounty. It was captured in the photos she took of bloom after beautiful bloom. I saw it in her hope-filled face as she tucked buckets of bulbs into the bare beds each season.

She never worked a day in the gardens of her great-grandmother or her grandfather Vivian, but sixty years later my mother can still recall the smell of rich, damp earth that would waft into their dining room from the nearby greenhouse on a warm summer day. Although she can't tell you the color of the spades they used, she can describe in vivid detail their colorful garden spaces where she would swing and run with her sister each summer.

I love how the robin showed Mary the way to *The Secret Garden*, but he didn't make her walk through the door. She did that all on her own. My hope is that you will now look around you with a fresh set of eyes and discover the good things that you want to grow in your own life and garden. To help you on this mission, on behalf of the family, I am proclaiming today that you are now an Official Secret Gardener. The seeds you choose to plant in your own backyard and heart are totally up to you.

Maytham Hall,
Rolvenden,
Kent.

Goodbye !

(Henry James thinking of
his tea.)

Frank Richmond Kimbrough drew Burnett's robin at the end of a visit to Maytham that had included tea with Henry James at his home in nearby Rye.

I want to encourage you to choose wisely. Choose kind words over angry ones. Plant goodness. Water what matters most, instead of the weeds. And tend consistently to your garden and life so they will grow into something that can inspire and uplift generations to come.

Blessings and Blooms,
Keri Wilt
TheWell-TendedLife.com

CHAPTER 1. THE LOCKED DOOR

"Cottonopolis" is a 19th-century nickname for the city of Manchester, the center of the cotton manufacturing industry in England. During Frances Hodgson's early childhood, the mills of the Manchester area were responsible for a third of global cotton production.

"So long as" TOI p. 254.

"Such lovely pictures!" TOI p. 24.

"the Violet stayed" TOI p. 25.

"*U* unable to" PUL/*The Alphabet of Flowers*, London: Dean & Son, 1850, p. 7.

"the back garden of Eden" TOI p. 29.

"There were roses" TOI p. 31.

"widowed ladies with" TOI p. 70.

"ugliest, smokiest factory" ITG p. 9.

"cattle-sheds for" Engels, Friedrich. *The Condition of the Working-class in England in 1844*, London: Swan Sonnenschein & Company, 1892, p. 51.

"a bit o' Yorkshire" TSG p. 234.

"adored the stories" TOI p. 253.

"up to the… Georges" TOI p. 114.

"At least it" TOI p. 255.

"It did not really matter" TOI p. 260.

"not a stranger" TOI p. 264.

"To get up" TOI p. 263.

"speak American," "I guess," "I reckon" TOI p. 262.

"What larks!" TRL p. 125.

"Shabbiness as a" From "Bohemia," quoted in GER p. 37.

"Temple of the" TOI p. 299.

"remuneration" TOI p. 286.

"Aunt Cynthy's girls" TOI p. 306.

"I have made gardens" ITG p. 10.

"Mammy Prissy" TRL p. 75.

"I want my" To Mary Bucklin Claflin, 14 July 1882, Overbury Collection of Barnard College Archives and Special Collections, quoted in GER p. 59.

"a strange wonderful" Leyda, Jay. *The Years and Hours of Emily Dickinson*, vol. 2, New Haven: Yale University Press, 1960, p. 322, quoting FHB to Myra (Mrs. F. P. Jordan), 7 April 1918, about a visit on 5 May 1880. Source of the original letter is unknown. See also WFP footnote for p. 64.

"Yes, I am reading" Louisa May Alcott to Mary Mapes Dodge, 9 January [1887]. PUL, the Wilkinson Collection of Mary Mapes Dodge. Note, FHB successfully sued in British court for copyright protection over the dramatization of *Little Lord Fauntleroy* in 1887; she was lauded for the decision by authors, both British and American.

"I never was" NYPL/FHB to RWG, 12 December 1876.

"[Lionel] is lying" NYPL/FHB to RWG, September 1877.

"once lived in" NYPL/FHB to EJ, 22 June 1922. In *Children I Have Known* (London: James R. Osgood, McIlvaine & Company, 1892, p. 92), Burnett wrote, "I was very intimate with the birds—quite on visiting terms. They used to perch on my window ledge sometimes and talk to each other about me, and they quarrelled with each other without the slightest embarrassment as they hopped about the branches. There was a lady sparrow who lived in a most fashionable nest at the very top and who used to scold her husband severely and chirp back at him like a vixen when he dared to answer her. I think she used to accuse him of bringing indigestible worms to his family, and say that a sparrow with the least proper domestic feeling would provide more carefully." Perhaps Burnett was projecting her marital issues on to her avian companions.

"odorous with the" PUL/FHB to VB, 1 April 1898. FHB lived in Washington well before the cherry tree planting around the Tidal Basin in 1912.

"le petit jeune" PUL/FHB to VB, undated, postmark 5 October 1890.

"At every second" PUL/FHB to VB, undated, postmark March 1891.

"Hampstead is really" PUL/FHB to VB, undated, possibly 1897.

"Nature never yet" Tucker, Terry. "Mrs. Hodgson Burnett's Bermuda Sojourn," *The Bermuda Historical Quarterly*, vol. 20, no. 4, Winter 1963, p. 112.

"I have reasoned" PUL/FHB to VB, 1 December 1895.

"Today is a" PUL/FHB to VB, 11 April 1895.

CHAPTER 2. FINDING THE KEY

The early history of Maytham Hall is based on the documentation for the property's Grade II heritage listing, entry number 1000221, available from historicengland.org.uk. According to a classified advertisement in *The [London] Standard*, 6 July 1895, p. 12, the estate was close to 900 acres, of which the mansion, gardens, and grounds made up 120 acres. Since then, the parcels have been sold, leaving the property at just over 100 acres.

"Next year my" PUL/FHB to VB, 22 July 1898.

"I wish you" PUL/FHB to VB, 28 February 1898.

"in the midst" PUL/FHB to VB, late July 1901.

"Oh, the agent" Harwood, Charlotte. "Mrs. Frances Hodgson Burnett at Home," *The Critic*, vol. 40, 1902, p. 232.

"The taking of," "Here began what" TRL p. 286.

"currants of all" PUL/FHB to VB, 22 July 1898.

"Next year the," "Bolton is a," "I have 'allowed," "by the dozen" PUL/FHB to VB, 5 June 1898.

"a red cotton" Carruth, Frances. "The Representative Woman's Point of View," *The St. Paul Globe*, magazine section, 10 January 1904, p. 1.

"One never knows" PUL/FHB to VB, 22 July 1898.

"In England nothing" PUL/FHB to VB, 1 April 1898.

"I shall have" PUL/FHB to EF, 30 September 1899.

"Dear Miss Fanton" Archives of American Art at the Smithsonian Institution, Mary Fanton Roberts papers, FHB to MFR, c.1905.

"turn Rolvenden into" PUL/FHB to EF, 2 May 1899.

"huge laughing parties" PUL/FHB to VB, June 1901.

"Frances indulged" In *The Indianapolis News*, on the subject of cigarette smoking by women, FHB was reported to have said "that the question was a personal one, and each woman must decide for herself whether she wished to smoke." 6 December 1910, p. 16.

"I have artfully" NYPL/FHB to RWG, c.1900.

"I've tried" Carruth p. 1.

"a major change" In the wedding announcement, which appeared in *The [London] Morning Post*, 15 March 1900, p. 5, Townesend is listed as F.R.C.S (Fellow of the Royal College of Medicine), although he was no longer practicing medicine at the time. Few images have survived of Stephen

Townesend, but another is reproduced in WFP, illustration insert pp. 164–165.

"I am obliged" PUL/FHB to EF, 30 May 1900.

"To get down" Carruth p. 1.

SPRING AT MAYTHAM

"Spring is a thing," "English weather is" PUL/FHB to EF, 2 May 1899.

"a catacomb of," "equinoctial gales" PUL/FHB to VB, 30 March 1901.

"The herbaceous plants" Carruth p. 1.

"sharp little pale" TSG p. 100.

"You want to" PUL/FHB to EF, 2 May 1899.

"Bolton has been," "Tere aint no" NYPL/FHB to RWG, 8 May 1910.

"We are waiting" PUL/FHB to EF, 2 May 1899.

SUMMER AT MAYTHAM

"The Rose Garden is," "there were no" PUL/FHB to EF, 12 June 1900.

"As long as," "unburdened [her] troubles" MFR p. 538.

"greedy beyond almost" MFR p. 546.

"cut the roses" PUL/FHB to EF, 12 June 1900.

"topped all its" MFR p. 545.

"I had boasted" PUL/SMN p. 11–6, FHB to Mr. [George] Boughton, c.1899.

"such people &" NYPL/FHB to RWG, 31 March 1901.

"carried about tea," "dispensed blocks of" NYPL/FHB to RWG, 10 August 1900.

"her outdoor sanctuary" The concept of "sanctuary," as connected to the garden at Maytham Hall, is introduced in HAE p. 149.

"How you would" PUL/SMN p. 11–7, FHB to VB, 9 June 1901.

AUTUMN AT MAYTHAM

"I cannot write," "The golden days," "This place is" PUL/FHB to VB, 22 September 1904.

"Darling Bolton" and the preceding mention of the numbers of bulbs expected, PUL/FHB to EF from Maytham Hall, undated.

"Guess what!" PUL/FHB to EF, 6 November [1898].

"dug & developed," "It may cause," "We dig it" PUL/FHB to EF, 30 September 1899.

"Burnett once referred" ITG p. 22.

"Oh the great" PUL/FHB to EF, 3 October 1908.

CHAPTER 3. A GARDENER'S GUIDE TO *THE SECRET GARDEN*

Details on the history and use of mistletoe are from "Mistletoe on High Altar: Ancient Observance at York Minster," a sermon preached 1 December 1929 by George Austen, reprinted in the *Yorkshire Herald*.

"In the hidden" PUL/SMN p. 18–11, FHB to William Heinemann, 9 October 1910.

"the most disagreeable-looking" TSG p. 1.

"as tyrannical and" TSG p. 2.

"Mistress Mary, quite," "Go away!" TSG p. 11.

"There's a big" TSG p. 18.

"It's just miles" TSG p. 26.

"still two miles" TSG p. 28.

"evergreens clipped into" TSG p. 42.

"trained flat against" TSG p. 43.

"breathing quite fast" TSG p. 96.

SPRING AT MISSELTHWAITE

"But she was *inside*" TSG p. 99.

"who had flown" TSG p. 98.

"It was the sweetest" TSG p. 97.

"One of the things" TSG pp. 97–98.

"sharp little pale," "Yes, they are" TSG p. 100.

"I wish—" TSG p. 104.

"In the shop" TSG p. 106.

"Our Dickon can" TSG p. 103.

"a sort of wood fairy" TSG p. 139.

"I am such friends" PUL/SMN p. 7–10, FHB to VB, c.1893.

"Eh! It is a queer" TSG p. 127.

"be friends with," "If they're thirsty" TSG p. 311.

"I wouldn't want" TSG p. 134.

"a bit of earth" TSG p. 148.

"When you see" TSG p. 149.

"The rain is" TSG p. 154.

"I have eight" PUL/SMN p. 3–25, FHB to VB from Switzerland, c.1897.

"something Magic," "It's warm—warm!" TSG p. 193.

"You never kiss" TSG p. 197.

"Things are crowding" TSG pp. 247–248.

SUMMER AT MISSELTHWAITE

"And the roses" TSG p. 296.

"to unfurl," "every shade of blue" TSG p. 295.

"a bed o' blue" TSG p. 254.

"always wanted blue" PUL/SMN p. 14–7.

"Rising out of" TSG p. 296.

AUTUMN AT MISSELTHWAITE

"Where you tend" TSG p. 355.

"Magic is in" TSG p. 301.

"Oh! the things" TSG p. 295.

"the Great Good Thing" PUL/FHB to VB, 14 October 1906.

"Good Thing," "[t]h' same thing" TSG p. 349.

"wonders of blue" TSG p. 357.

"In the wonderful" PUL/FHB to VB, 1 June 1910.

"In the garden" TSG p. 361.

"The place was," "going to live" TSG p. 372.

"was our Rose" PUL/SMN p. 18–2, FHB to Ella Hepworth Dixon, undated.

"A children's Jane Eyre" PUL/SMN p. 18–11, FHB to William Heinemann, 9 October 1910.

CHAPTER 4. NEST BUILDING

William Tachau, the architect that Frances and Vivian Burnett employed for Plandome Park, also designed the neoclassical Naumburg Bandshell in New York City's Central Park.

"Her garden was" TSG p. 153.

"It will be nice" PUL/FHB to EF, 8 August 1908.

"Some sources indicate" GER p. 335, footnote 13.

"Millions of money" PUL/FHB to EF, 3 October 1908.

"seething, boiling, blasting" PUL/FHB to EF, 29 August 1913.

"I have decided" PUL/FHB to VB, 29 April 1910.

"Famous Novelist" *The Times-Dispatch*, 28 July 1911, p. 5.

"only a little garden" ITG p. 28.

"Eh! the nests," "It'd be th' safest" TSG p. 129.

"magnificent emperors of" NYPL/FHB to EJ, undated.

"our salvation in" PUL/FHB to VB, 1 June 1920.

"Land of the Blue Flower" was the title of one of her children's stories (New York: Moffat, Yard & Company, 1916). On 8 April 1917, the *Des Moines Register* published a undated letter from FHB to the seventh-grade class of the Hubbell School in which she wrote, "I am sending you a picture of myself in my Land of the Blue Flower, which is what I call a garden I made with delphiniums and roses. My face is in the shade and you cannot see me very clearly, but there I am under the rose arch with a basket of blue flowers on my arm."

"Those long spires" TSG p. 240.

"delphiniums in later" PUL/SMN pp. 14–7 to 8.

"A comfortable, rambling" Overton, Grant. *The Women Who Make Our Novels*, New York: Moffat, Yard & Company, 1919, p. 360.

"When a new" From "Takes Delight in Gardens," *Lexington* [VA] *Gazette*, 3 July 1912, p. 6.

"Please replace some" PUL/FHB to VB, 12 May 1920.

"Welcome Bed" Undated list of roses by FHB, MS.2266, University of Tennessee Libraries, Knoxville, Special Collections.

"harmonizes well with" Maxwell, Henry. "Gardening Under Glass," *Country Life in America*, vol. 22, 15 August 1912, p. 34.

"Is the greenhouse" PUL/FHB to VB from Penshurst, Kent, May 1910.

"*IMPORTANT. Are* the" PUL/FHB to VB, undated, postmark August 1918.

"respectable persons whose" Ettinger, George T. "Life and Letters Literary Gossip," *Allentown [PA] Morning Call*, 26 September 1911.

"master's work" PUL/SMN p. 14–10.

"so quietly entertaining" *The Progressive Farmer and Southern Farm Gazette*, 12 October 1912.

"Dear Little Namesake" PUL/SMN pp. 20–3 to 4.

"bloom next summer" PUL/SMN p. 18–3, FHB to Frederick Stokes, 6 November 1911.

CHAPTER 5. A NEW BIT OF EARTH

"Roses & lilies" PUL/FHB to VB undated, postmark 13 March 1911.

"When she leaves" Overton, Grant. *The Women Who Make Our Novels*, New York: Moffat, Yard & Company, 1919, pp. 357–365.

"I have had" PUL/FHB to VB, 18 June 1921.

"The Acalifa," "Have you ever" PUL/FHB to VB, 23 January 1912.

"imperiously" Tucker, Terry. "Mrs. Hodgson Burnett's Bermuda Sojourn," *The Bermuda Historical Quarterly*, vol. 20, no. 4, Winter 1963, p. 113.

"chick o' the village" PUL/FHB to VB, 23 March 1921.

"the place where" PUL/FHB to Verity and Dorinda Burnett, c.1920.

"almost as intimate" PUL/FHB to VB, 23 March 1921.

"No one on" PUL/EF to FHB, undated fragment from Bermuda, c.1915.

"pen-driving machine" TRL p. 75.

"she expects herself" Hills, William H., editor. "Personal Gossip About Authors," *The Writer*, vol. 25, no. 7, July 1913, p. 106.

"As we drove" PUL/FHB to VB, 29 November 1920.

"I shall stay" PUL/SMN pp. 12–10 to 12, FHB to Ella and Madge Hepworth Dixon, 29 December 1912.

"One can find" NYPL/FHB to EJ, 15 September 1915.

"From Leaf to Leaf" *Harper's Magazine*, vol. 137, November 1918, p. 797.

"The birds will sing" PUL/SMN p. 15–12, FHB to Rosamund Campbell, 16 November 1918.

"I foresee that" PUL/FHB to VB, 17 November 1913.

"It seems strange" PUL/FHB to VB, 26 April 1916. "Green points" must have been a favorite phrase: it appears nine times in *The Secret Garden*.

"very savage," "I am afraid" PUL/FHB to VB from Bermuda, undated.

"Woman Suffrage Party" *The New York Times*, reporting on a suffrage flower sale on Lower Broadway to benefit the cause, noted that "flowers from Mrs. Frances Hodgson Burnett's famous blue garden [were] brought in from Long Island early yesterday morning," 23 June 1914, p. 11.

"the visitors who" NYPL/FHB to EJ, 22 August 1919. For example, the *New York Tribune* reported on 1 July 1923 that "to aid the Wayside Home for Girls at Valley Stream, Mrs. Frances Hodgson Burnett will throw open her estate, Plandome Park, Plandome, L.I., to the public on Saturday, July 7, from 2 to 6 p.m. Tea will be served in the garden to visitors. Mrs. Burnett is said to know intimately every flower and shrub on her estate, and working among them is her daily occupation."

"they will go" PUL/FHB to Clarence Clough Buel, 16 July 1914.

"Sneak Garden" PUL/SMN p. 14–7.

"I am Nanda," "There is Mr." NYPL/FHB to EJ, undated.

CHAPTER 6. WHEN THE SUN WENT DOWN

"As long as one" ITG p. 10.

"I call feebly" PUL/FHB to VB, 24 February 1921.

"The explanation of" PUL/FHB to VB, 24 March 1921.

"cold brave flowers," "The wonderful varied" NYPL/FHB to EJ from Plandome Park, undated.

"little house," "The repairer of" Burnett, Vivian. "She Wrote Fauntleroy" (undated typed manuscript), p. 71, quoting FHB to VB, 23 January 1912.

"He is a Gardener" NYPL/FHB to EJ, 26 June 1922.

"belong to the," "she wrote lyrically" *The New York Times*, magazine section, 4 December 1927, p. 10.

CHAPTER 7. FURTHER GARDEN WRITINGS OF FRANCES HODGSON BURNETT

"AN AMERICAN AUTHOR'S ENGLISH HA-HA"

Concerning FHB's nationality, in *The Journal of Education*, vol. 84–85, 27 September 1917, p. 289, she is quoted as saying "I am not English. I am both English and American. I am more of one until the other in me is denied and then I am that; and taken altogether, if I were not English, I should not be American; if not American, not English."

"Mrs. Burnett has" From "Literary Notes," *The Baltimore Sun*, 4 July 1906, p. 7.

"Burnett once mentioned" PUL/FHB to Rosamund Campbell, undated.

"*Have* I told" PUL/FHB to EF, 2 May 1899.

MY ROBIN

"with roses and" NYPL/Annie Russell Papers (MssCol302), box 1, folder 4, FHB to Annie Russell, 1 September 1899.

"In correspondence with" PUL/SMN p. 18–12, FHB to Frederick Stokes, 6 March 1911.

"Even old Barton's" Burnett's head gardener at Maytham Hall was her "Darling Bolton," not Barton. Perhaps she changed the name to honor his privacy.

IN THE GARDEN

"Can't we talk" Carruth, Frances. "The Representative Woman's Point of View," *The St. Paul Globe*, magazine section, 10 January 1904, p. 1.

"Pusley is worse" Pusley (or purslane) is a common name for *Portulaca oleracea*, a fast-growing annual weed.

CHAPTER 8. FRANCES'S PLANTS

"Of course I" NYPL/FHB to EJ, 26 June 1922.

"I couldna' say" TSG p. 254.

AFTERWORD

"And the secret" TSG p. 328.

"Will you show" TSG p.122.

"If I had" TSG p. 105.

Just as my gardens are packed with plants from friends and fellow gardeners, this book is replete with contributions from individuals north, south, and around the Atlantic to whom I extend heartfelt thanks:

In memory of Gail Reuben and Jane Taylor, two dear friends who loved *The Secret Garden* and separately encouraged me to write this book. You are both still with me every step of the way.

Hazel Beany, gardener at Great Maytham Hall, who generously shared her knowledge of Burnett, the plants in the gardens, and the local history of Rolvenden.

Leigh and Doug Conant, whose secret garden on Green Avenue in Madison, New Jersey, was its own blooming enclosure of joy.

Donald Davidson, who identified and described Burnett's luxury automobile in the period photograph of her Plandome Park garage.

Yolanda Fundora, whose unerring eye and artistic skill made the illustrations sing.

Linda O'Gorman, Sandra Swan, and Pamela Zave, whose corrections and suggestions improved the manuscript immensely.

Barry Thomson, architectural historian, who unearthed so much information about the Burnett residences in Long Island.

David Wheeler, editor of *Hortus*, who encouraged my interest in Burnett by accepting an article for the Autumn 2017 issue of his unrivaled journal.

To the archivists and librarians who preserve the source materials on which my research is wholly dependent, including—

The staff of Princeton University Library, Manuscripts Division, Department of Special Collections, with special shout-outs to AnnaLee Pauls, and Andrea

Immel, curator of the Cotsen Children's Library, for her assistance in identifying Frances Hodgson's floral alphabet book;

Tal Nadan, Reference Archivist, Manuscripts and Archives Division, New York Public Library, and the staff of the Brooke Russell Astor Reading Room;

Tema Hecht at the New York Public Library for the Performing Arts;

George Boziwick, emeritus Chief of the Music Division, New York Public Library for the Performing Arts;

Stephen Sinon, William B. O'Connor Curator of Special Collections, Research and Archives, Esther Jackson, Public Services Librarian, and the ever-helpful staff of the Plant Information Desk, The LuEsther T. Mertz Library of the New York Botanical Garden;

Kelly Crawford, Museum Specialist, Collections, Education and Access, Archives of American Gardens, Smithsonian Institution;

Kyle Hovious, Special Collections, Hodges Library, University of Tennessee;

Karla Ingemann, Records Officer, Bermuda Archives, Hamilton, Bermuda;

Leora Siegel, Senior Director, Lenhardt Library, Chicago Botanic Garden;

Natalie Toy, Heritage Assistant, The Old Palace, Dean's Park, York, United Kingdom;

Penny White, Reference Librarian, Albert & Shirley Small Special Collections Library, University of Virginia.

My friends and colleagues at Timber Press, long may you reign.

Jenny Bent—first, best, and only agent.

And Kirke Bent, listed last, but never least.

PHOTO & ILLUSTRATION CREDITS

Pages 6, 49, 53, 90. Frances Benjamin Johnston Photograph Collection, The Huntington Library, San Marino, California.

Pages 8, 50 (left). Yolanda Fundora.

Page 10. Book cover from *The Secret Garden* by Frances Hodgson Burnett— Illustrated by Tasha Tudor. Illustration copyright © 1962 by J. B. Lippincott Company. Illustration copyright © renewed 1990 by HarperCollins Publishers. Used by permission of HarperCollins Publishers.

Pages 19, 268. Princeton University Library, Department of Rare Books and Special Collections, Cotsen Children's Library.

Page 26. Iva Villi / Shutterstock.

Pages 29, 77, 112, 142, 270. Rare Book Collection of the Lenhardt Library of the Chicago Botanic Garden.

Pages 29, 33 (left), 36, 43, 55, 62, 63, 84, 162, 191, 192, 218, 288. Princeton University Library, Department of Rare Books and Special Collections.

Pages 33 (right), 37 (left), 145, 153, 155, 166 (top), 171 (left), 195, 202. The History Center at the Manhattan Public Library.

Pages 34, 45, 158, 179, 180 (right), 195 (top), 214. Rob Cardillo.

Page 38. Boston Athenaeum.

Page 40. © National Portrait Gallery, London.

Pages 51, 54, 60, 65, 70, 74 (right), 78–79, 82, 86, 89, 92 (top), 94–95, 97, 98, 99, 101, 104–105, 135, 136, 171 (right), 189, 209, 229. Suzie Gibbons.

Pages 64, 68, 190, 284. Special Collections, New York Public Library for the Performing Arts.

Page 67. Rowland Cole / Shutterstock.

Page 92 (bottom). © The Board of Trustees of the Royal Botanic Gardens, Kew.

Page 102. Smithsonian Institution, Archives of American Gardens.

Pages 116 (right), 128. Graham Rust / Breslich & Foss.

Page 118. From *The Secret Garden*. Illustrations © 2007 Inga Moore. Reproduced by permission of the publisher, Candlewick Press, on behalf of Walker Books, London.

Pages 144, 161, 194, 201, 205. The LuEsther T. Mertz Library of the New York Botanical Garden.

Pages 164 (left), 180 (left). Rob Cardillo / W. A. Burpee.

Pages 164–165. University of Tennessee, Knoxville, Special Collections.

Page 174. Michael Halbert, Illustration.

Page 177. Frances Benjamin Johnston, Portrait, Frances Hodgson Burnett, between 1890 and 1910. Photograph, Library of Congress, Prints and Photographs Division, Frances Benjamin Johnston Collection, loc.gov/pictures/item/2002697460.

Page 183. Kenneth D. Johnson.

Page 184. MSantana618 / Shutterstock.

Pages 186, 203. Manuscripts and Archives Division, New York Public Library.

Page 198. Scott McKowen.

Page 213. Book cover from *The Secret Garden* (Illustrated with interactive elements) by Frances Hodgson Burnett. Illustrations copyright © 2018 by MinaLima Ltd. Used by permission of HarperCollins Publishers.

All other photographs and images are either by the author, from the author's collection, or in the public domain.

INDEX

311

M

magic, 31, 60, 118, 130, 137, 141, 238

Malus domestica, 274

Manchester area, 18–19, 21–23, 24, 26–27, 290n

manure, 100, 177

maple, 35

marigold, 163, 179, 265, 266, 275, 278

"Mary, Mary quite contrary", 111, 113

Maytham Hall
  acreage, 292n
  after FHB's tenure, 103, 105
  comparisons with Misselthwaite, 114–115, 170
  FHB's reasons for buying, 48–49, 52
  locale, 49–51, 59, 60
  Ordnance Survey map, 50
  sale of, 100–101

Maytham Hall garden. *See also* rose garden
  after FHB's tenure, 51, 82, 86, 89, 101–102, 135–136, 209, 210–211
  autumn landscape, 92–93, 96–99
  Bolton (gardener), 56, 57, 58, 59–60, 80–81, 85–86

brick walls, 85, 94, 171, 282

bulbs, 73, 76, 80, 96–97, 228

Fairy Wood, 64, 76, 85

ha-ha, 221–222, 226–228

kitchen gardens, 54

old orchard, 59–60, 83–84

rehabilitation and improvements, 56, 59–60, 100

soil enrichment, 99–100

spring landscape, 72–81

summer landscape, 83, 85–86

terrace, 53, 56, 64

trees, 52, 81, 114–115, 117

winter to spring transition, 71–72

Maytham Maniacs, 62, 63

Medlock, Mrs. (fictional character), 113–114

Mexican fireweed, 278

mignonette, 134, 201, 279

Miller, Lynden B., 212

Misselthwaite Manor (fictional setting)
  autumn landscape, 141, 145–146
  bulbs, 73, 120–122, 130
  comparisons with Maytham Hall, 114–115, 170
  house and staff, 113–117
  locale, 114